The American Assembly, *Columbia University*

THE ECONOMY
AND THE PRESIDENT:
1980 AND BEYOND

Prentice-Hall, Inc., *Englewood Cliffs, New Jersey*
A SPECTRUM BOOK

Library of Congress Cataloging in Publication Data
Main entry under title:

THE ECONOMY AND THE PRESIDENT.

(A Spectrum Book)
At head of title: The American Assembly, Columbia
University.
Background papers, edited by W. E. Hoadley, prepared
for the American Assembly held Mar. 6–8, 1980 at the
Center for Study of the American Experience.
Includes index.
1. United States—Economic conditions—1971–
—Addresses, essays, lectures. 2. United States—
Economic policy—1971– —Addresses, essays, lectures.
3. Presidents—United States—Addresses, essays,
lectures. I. Hoadley, Walter Evans, (date).
II. American Assembly.
HC106.7.E328   338.973   80-17443
ISBN 0-13-234823-3
ISBN 0-13-234815-2 (pbk.)

Chapter 3 is used by permission of Otto Eckstein, president of
Data Resources, Inc.

Table 1 on page 80 is from Edward F. Denison, *Accounting for
Slower Economic Growth: The United States in the 1970s* (Washington, D.C.: Brookings Institution, 1979), Table 7-3. Copyright 1979
by the Brookings Institution. Reprinted by permission.

Editorial/production supervision by Betty Neville
Manufacturing buyer: Barbara A. Frick

10 9 8 7 6 5 4 3 2 1

PRENTICE-HALL INTERNATIONAL, INC. (*London*)
PRENTICE-HALL OF AUSTRALIA PTY. LIMITED (*Sydney*)
PRENTICE-HALL OF CANADA, LTD. (*Toronto*)
PRENTICE-HALL OF INDIA PRIVATE LIMITED (*New Delhi*)
PRENTICE-HALL OF JAPAN, INC. (*Tokyo*)
PRENTICE-HALL OF SOUTHEAST ASIA PTE. LTD. (*Singapore*)
WHITEHALL BOOKS LIMITED (*Wellington, New Zealand*)

Table of Contents

Preface

When the United States entered upon the decade of the seventies, political leaders were divided in their views about the most effective measures to pursue in the management of the American economy. These divisions reflected different political and philosophical attitudes toward governance of the American commonwealth, but they all had one thing in common: the conviction by their protagonists that the American economy was manageable.

As we enter the decade of the eighties, more and more Americans are beginning to question whether our economy is manageable. Some observers have suggested that our economy is "over the hill" and that we must either undertake fundamental changes to our whole system or else face the prospect of becoming a second-rate nation, watching others take over the primacy of world economic leadership.

In order to address this prospect, the Center for Study of the American Experience, The Annenberg School of Communications, sponsored an American Assembly on "Economic Issues and the President: 1980 and Beyond." A group of distinguished Americans met at the Center from March 6 to 8, 1980, to participate in this Assembly. Walter E. Hoadley, chief economist for the Bank of America, acted as director, and, under his editorial supervision, background papers were prepared for the use of the participants. These papers have been compiled into the present volume, which is published as a stimulus to further thinking about the discussion of this subject among informed and concerned citizens. It is the hope of the Center and of The American Assembly that a consensus may develop among the American electorate which will be responsive to presidential leadership in the decisions which must be taken to enhance the prospects for our national economy in this decade.

The opinions expressed in this volume are those of the individual authors and not necessarily those of The American Assembly, nor the Center for Study of the American Experience, neither of which institution takes a stand on the topics it presents for public discussion.

William H. Sullivan
President
The American Assembly

Walter E. Hoadley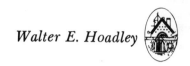

Introduction

The 1980s promises to be a decade of destiny for the United States. The decisions to be made in 1980 and beyond by the President of the United States, other national leaders, and the American people will determine our future for generations to come.

Our nation now is at a crucial turning point—in part because the world around is changing rapidly, but also because we have largely refused to face squarely the major problems of our times: weakening public confidence, inflation, energy, capital investment, productivity, fiscal deficits, monetary discipline, international trade and payments imbalances, weak dollar, public-private sector conflicts, youth unemployment, and more.

In many respects we wasted the decade of the 1970s in doubt, debate, drift, and dissension. We made few positive decisions and demonstrated little national determination to resolve critical issues. We clearly cannot afford similarly to waste the 1980s. Too much of our way of life is at stake.

The policies and goals of the past seem far short of what is

WALTER E. HOADLEY *is executive vice president and chief economist of the Bank of America. On the bank's managing committee, he directs economics, policy research, and related strategic activities world-wide. Mr. Hoadley was previously chairman of the Federal Reserve Bank of Philadelphia and vice president and treasurer of Armstrong Cork Company. Mr. Hoadley is active in a wide variety of U.S. and international business and professional groups. He also serves as an officer and advisor to many government agencies, universities, and religious organizations.*

needed to cope with the unprecedented changes ahead, enduring as well as cyclical.

The President of the United States will have primary responsibility to be our catalyst—to motivate and lead our nation through what are apt to be turbulent times in such a way that we emerge a stronger, more unified, and more confident people. He will need all the help he can get. The main task will be to convince many doubting citizens and innumerable others abroad that our future is much brighter than commonly judged, that we can and will solve our key problems, that we will accept inconveniences and sacrifices that are needed for success.

The problems we now face are not new. There are no real surprises. Moreover, they are not going to disappear soon. Nor will they solve themselves.

There are no quick or easy answers as much as we might like them. The roots of our major problems are fairly deep. They have been developing slowly but relentlessly for more than a decade. The principal root seems to be Americans' longstanding desire to help people—reinforced by a political goal to win votes. Americans generally have wanted to help the underprivileged improve their living standards and to find a place in the mainstream of our society. In the background, of course, has been a depression-born public fervor to put idle people and idle resources to work.

The main U.S. problem of the past—unemployment—is not the main problem today or tomorrow. It is inflation that is now our greatest economic threat, without minimizing the personal tragedy of unemployment.

The overwhelming emphasis of U.S. economic policy for years has been to stimulate *demand* while taking *supply* pretty much for granted, except during defense emergencies. Supply of labor and materials almost always has seemed to be in abundance. Moreover, the policy implications have been that investment, output, productivity, savings, and research and development—all vital dimensions of supply management policy—are far less important, and sometimes even unimportant. Contributing to the adverse effects have been the repeated political pronouncements that profits, and capital gains in particular, are mostly ill-gotten and really of benefit only to relatively few privileged people and not the general public.

We now know that most of the population is affected by what happens to supply as well as demand. If the President doesn't take more steps promptly to achieve a better balance between supply and demand in the U.S., most of our problems can only intensify.

The consequences of demand policies and developments through the years have finally begun to emerge as powerful negative depressant forces in our society. The prevailing consumption-motivated political-regulatory process has promised better, safer, less risky, more secure personal living, but in fact has steadily eroded the underpinnings of precisely these conditions.

The principal innovators, risk takers, entrepreneurs, investors, savers, and tireless managers and workers with solid confidence in the longer-range future of our nation have all become fewer. Ironically, those who continue to have strong positive views about our nation's future often have enough doubts themselves now to want a quicker higher return on their new investments. This means that the minimum acceptable rate of return, especially in our atmosphere of high inflation, rises more and more in a self-constricting cycle, progressively limiting needed risk taking and investment. This is a dangerous cycle and obviously must be broken by some major changes in U.S. economic and related policies if we are to sustain reasonable growth and living standards as well as provide challenging opportunities for our people.

Far more attention and encouragement must be given to supply management and improvement—in order to make it possible to enlarge and preserve demand across our land in the remainder of this century.

Unhappily, our national decision making process has become more and more crisis oriented. Currently we seem to lack the ability to reach a consensus on most major problems until and unless there is an undeniable crisis which calls unmistakably for action. Our priorities are therefore mainly determined by crisis. Our policies increasingly are late and reactive rather than early and anticipating. The President must provide more creative direction.

Striving for domestic full employment—however necessary—is no longer a sufficient goal for the United States, in considerable measure because at least technical full employment has been experienced without much, if any, evidence of real public satisfaction. Moreover, many able-bodied are not at work.

We must somehow get on with the task of resolving other equally critical problems. The same process must involve all sectors—first, in finding more agreement on what our principal priorities must be (if we have to use the ballot box to poll the nation to find out), and second, in developing new ways to coordinate many separate and often conflicting efforts to achieve desired results in both our national and individual interest.

Whatever our convictions, we can no longer afford to hold out for single or theoretically pure courses of action. The President must bring us together through more pragmatic compromises to move our economy ahead. We cannot wait endlessly for perfection to materialize in policies or programs. We must choose our major goal or goals carefully, set a specific course, and move ahead, refining if necessary as we go along, but never losing sight of our prime objective—to combat inflation!

Business and government in the U.S. must find ways to reach more understanding in their interrelations to meet the challenges, if not attacks, of concerted programs aimed at American interests and markets from abroad.

Government regulators must seek and become directly accountable for correcting the negative cost-benefits of their efforts, however well intentioned.

Business leaders must become far better informed on the practical aspects of political decision making, which is always complex.

Academics must be more willing to subject their theories to the test of the real world and revise or abandon them if they fall short of expectations.

Labor must accept the principle that productivity gains set an inevitable limit on wage and salary increases if inflation is to be reduced and held in check.

The United States simply cannot ignore the need for sustained economic growth, the vigorous supply essentials for achieving such growth, or the devastating effects of permitting inflation to get worse or even remain close to the world level if we are to preserve our living standards and retain a marked degree of world leadership.

Highly important, we must now give much more precedence to resolving issues of great national importance and be more willing to subserve others because our nation's future—and therefore our personal futures—are threatened. The President and the Congress must ask what are the national consequences of their principal actions for our future—not just today. Are we adding to our basic strengths, or are we taking more out of our economy than we are putting back? If the latter, we really cannot afford to continue what we are doing because the inflationary impact will only compound the basic problems we so urgently need to resolve.

At this turning point in U.S. history, one question overshadows all others: has the United States permanently reached the zenith of its political and economic power?

No one, of course, should expect our country to regain the unchallenged position it had immediately after World War II. Then most of the world was devastated, and a massive political vacuum existed which no other nation could possibly fill.

Many people currently ask whether the United States can maintain a dynamic, powerful, and widely respected place in the modern day world of 1980 and beyond. There are some obviously strong feelings in many world capitals as well as at home that the United States cannot do so—because it is deemed to be definitely "over the hill."

If the United States really were "over the hill," much more than prestige would be at stake for Americans.

Internationally, we could hardly escape more widespread challenges and overtures against U.S. policies and interests, rising political tensions, more prolonged negotiations whenever U.S. public and private leaders seek agreements important to the American people, and more reluctance among foreigners to join with or follow us in concerted programs unless we are prepared to underwrite them in full.

Domestically, being in fact "over the hill" could only mean: chronically slower-to-actually declining growth, accelerating payments for foreign goods and services by transfer of U.S. owned tangible assets rather than almost entirely in dollars as in the past, gradual realization that individuals and families across our country must expect less and less in the future rather than the traditional American more and more, undoubtedly greater divisiveness and social tensions, higher inflation, and more unemployment, crime, and moral decay.

All this sounds like the scenario of a fallen leader of nations.

Can this be the United States? Certainly no President can agree.

The rationale for the United States being "over the hill" is usually given in such terms as our: lack of strong leadership in the Presidency and elsewhere, unwillingness to take the necessary disciplinary measures to check inflation or conserve energy, disregard of our increasing dependence upon other nations for energy and similar vital materials, unconcern about declining U.S. productivity, poor workmanship and noncompetitive quality in products and services, diminished interest in taking new risks and promoting innovation, inability to reach national consensus on key issues, weak political party loyalty, "paper tiger" defenses and unreliability as an ally, contentment to rest comfortably on our past accomplishments in many fields, and general apathy toward accepting further responsibility for forceful direction of world affairs.

Recent reports of public opinion across our country indicate that the over the hill view is not limited to offshore critics. Half or more of U.S. adults are said to believe that they have reached the peak of their living standards for many years to come and probably for their entire lifetimes.

Taken literally, this would mean that the end of the American dream is at hand. Tomorrow will no longer be better for us, our children, and grandchildren, in contrast to what generations of Americans have traditionally believed and proved by their own experience to be true.

If these negative expressions accurately reflect the deep feelings of many people toward the future of the United States, there is ample reason now for the President and every citizen to have real concern about what lies ahead in 1980 and beyond. Lack of confidence in our national future means lack of confidence in ourselves and has the potential of becoming self-fulfilling prophecy.

Perhaps our vast economic accomplishments have dulled our desires for further tangible goods and services. But, the goods we possess and services we use came largely from an era of cheap energy and virtually planned obsolescence and waste, because shortages were few and our policies called for massive efforts to put idle people and resources to work at almost any cost.

The era we face in the 1980s will be vastly different. We don't want (and frankly we cannot expect) repetition of past policies. What we do want now are much better goods and services which use far less energy and fit into a new world capitalizing upon more conservation, development, and productivity to give us a better quality of life while leading others to improve theirs.

In the 1980s we must replace a very large fraction of what we now use. This is a mammoth task and will require enormous new capital and technology. We must accomplish this improvement goal simultaneously with sustainable national growth and less inflation through highly motivated and rewarded men and women who strongly believe what they are doing is in our *common* interest as well as our personal interest.

As I read the 1980s, it's a time for a "we" generation to forge to the front of leadership. The motivation will come from:

1. Much greater recognition of our inherent national, personal, and management strengths;
2. Widespread observation that billions of people around the world aspire to what we now have, with hundreds of thousands actually coming to our country annually to participate in economic, social, and political benefits which most Americans do not appreciate;
3. The stark reality that our living standards, prestige, and ability to defend ourselves now depend upon an extended successful period of determined economic rearmament and some unavoidable military rearmament as well; and
4. The reawakening of American pride in accomplishment among younger as well as older citizens.

The pendulum of power in the United States is swinging relentlessly back toward grass roots America. In recent decades, voters have become rather disillusioned with leadership in all walks of U.S. life. A majority forcefully wants to have a much greater impact on the shaping of our future. Our democratic system still offers the opportunity to change what people don't like and to bring about what they do. The decade of the 1980s will witness one of the greatest groundswells in history of increased voter participation in our economic and political life. The President must be closer than ever to the people and lead.

The average United States citizen clearly wants to know much more about the problems we confront, even though most are already pretty well informed; the choices and sacrifices we have to make to resolve these problems; and how we can get on with the job. The President must provide these answers forcefully.

The chapters which follow point the way. They go well down the road toward providing the American public what it tells us it wants to know about the challenges facing the United States in the 1980s—our decade of destiny.

Daniel Yankelovich

1

Economic Policy
and the Question of Political Will

Introduction

In confronting the problem of inflation, economists find themselves handicapped by a peculiar difficulty. It comes, ironically, from one of the field's own greatest strengths. The growing power of econometric models makes them curiously awkward in dealing with the noneconomic aspects of inflation. Never have econometric models been more comprehensive in encompassing the intricate web of factors that make up the American economy. But they achieve this power partly through a narrowing of scope; that is, the equations of the econometric models encompass few of the noneconomic political, social, and psychological facets of the inflation problem. Unfortunately, however, the passage of time swells these issues to ever greater importance.

DANIEL YANKELOVICH *is president of Yankelovich, Skelly, and White, a public attitude research firm, and of the Public Agenda Foundation, a nonprofit organization founded to encourage public involvement in national policy issues. He is also a member of the Conference Board's Economic Forum. The author wishes to acknowledge the significant contributions made to this chapter by Larry Kaagan, a senior research associate of Yankelovich, Skelly, and White.*

It is a well-accepted fact that scientific and professional disciplines advance and refine themselves according to timetables dictated more by the dynamics within the field than by the urgency of practical problems in the real world. Improved concepts, new techniques, and the idiosyncrasies of leading personalities in the discipline are more often responsible for advances within a field than any need for solutions expressed by those outside the field. If the troublesome problems that beset the world fail to respect the lines drawn by the academic specialties, so much the worse for the problems. And so, we encounter one of those odd disparities that spring up from time to time in the history of thought: an academic discipline finds itself moving in one direction, while the perplexing and crucial problems that constitute its subject matter move in the opposite direction. Rarely in modern times has a wider gap opened up between the development of a professional field and the needs of its applied subject. The more capable economics becomes in precise measurement of the economic domain, the less able it is to take into systematic account the so-called "exogenous variables," i.e., everything that is not economics in a fairly strict sense.

Astute economists acknowledge these cross-pressures wistfully and with good humor. As individuals they go to great pains to make up for the field's technical limitations: in their work they take into account the political, social, and psychological aspects of the inflation problem, and they do so skillfully. But they do not bring to the task the systematic thoroughness that characterizes their formal models of economic activity. They analyze the economic aspects of inflation within one framework and then switch to another framework, that of the shrewd observer, to register the noneconomic influences. This deployment of a dual framework has led to a formulation heard with increasing frequency in the past few years that goes something like this: "We economists have the technical knowledge and the economic tools necessary to control inflation; what is lacking is the *political will* to put those tools to work."

This formulation appears to represent a fairly widespread conviction among leading economists and other observers. It is a handy way of summing up the supposed relationship between the economic facets of the inflation problem. Economists can figure out, within reason, which fiscal and monetary strategies will bring inflation under control. At that point it is up to the politicians and the country at large. If we as a nation have the guts to do what needs to be done, then we can deflate the worst of the inflationary pressures. If we lack the political will, then all the expert economic knowledge in the world will do us no good. This proposition is a true thought-stopper. It is plausible and has the ring of simple truth to it. It almost never elicits any further questions about what exactly is meant by political will or the lack of it; and as with all effective thought-stoppers, people rarely pause to think in what respects, if any, the proposition may be misleading.

The notion of "failed political will" can best be seen as a species of the growing fear described by Walter Hoadley in his introduction to this volume, that perhaps the United States, both as a dynamic economic force and as an international trading partner and world actor, has reached its zenith and begun its decline. Whether references are made to our falling productivity, our failure to curb our imports of oil from the Middle East, our decline in entrepreneurial innovation, or the growth of power of other nations, there is a prevalent wave of concern that our period of eminence might lie behind us. As the British historian Paul Johnson has observed, there was "a period of twenty-five to thirty years of American cultural-economic-military dominance, followed by what we are living through at the moment, a period of doubt and questioning which is going on all over the world."

"Failed political will" also conjures up imagery of a nation grown morally flabby and indecisive. It suggests, as President Carter suggested in his July 1979 "crisis of confidence" speech, that somehow Americans are newly lacking in willpower, that we have become mired in self-indulgence, and that the American genius for devising practical solutions to difficult problems has failed us in the face of perplexing new circumstances. The country is accused of suffering from a "malaise" that is moral in origin. In Mr. Carter's scolding of the American people we hear echoes of the currently fashionable theory (i.e., Christopher Lasch's *The Culture of Narcissism*) that the American character has changed for the worse, with Americans growing ever more preoccupied with their own selfish desires, more narcissistic, more self-centered. Some years ago, Tom Wolfe slapped the label "the me decade" on the 1970s, and it stuck.

In the current climate of opinion, the theory of failed political will as an explanation of our inflation problem sounds self-evident. It is only when we examine the changing social/political environment empirically that we come to understand how misleading it is. There is even a sense in which the fight against inflation is being hampered by an *excess* of political will, rather than a dearth of it. In what ways, we shall explore later in this chaper.

The economists who sense that a noneconomic factor holds the key to victory over inflation are correct, but they have, I believe, mislabeled the factor. They see the nation paralyzed by its failure to develop a coherent energy policy, improve its international competitiveness, revive its earlier post World War II record of substantial and steady productivity gains, resist pressures to hold down spending that favors special interest groups, and they attribute this paralysis to a failure of political will.

My own analysis of public opinion has led me to conclude that the cause of this paralysis is not failed will. Rather, it is a breakdown in consensus, which is quite another matter. As Thorstein Veblen argued more than a half century ago, the laws of economics are not fixed and independent but depend on the value system of the society. When social values change, economic guideposts must change accordingly. For many years our society was held together by an unspoken consensus that the economic imperative should prevail over virtually all competing values. Few questioned the wisdom of giving economic values—GNP growth, jobs, an ever-increasing standard of living—top priority. Economic policy makers were able to presuppose political support for whatever means were needed to reach our economic goals.

Today, however, the old consensus is frayed and fragmented at two different levels. Among opinion leaders ideological positions have hardened. The cleavages among contending groups holding different values have grown deeper. Business leaders, environmentalists, pro- and anti-nuclear factions, pro- and anti-regulatory factions, spokespeople for the women's movement and the minorities, quality-of-life proponents, and redistributionists who care more about how the pie is cut than how big it is, all bring different agendas of values to bear on the political process. And they do so with increasing effectiveness, exercising their political will skillfully on behalf of the values they hold most dear.

Among the general public there is widespread confusion and distrust. Americans have been hit hard by recent changes in the economy and in the culture and have not yet "taken them in." In principle, Americans are prepared to make choices, if necessary, but they are not yet convinced that such choices are needed. They do not trust those who tell them that they must sacrifice; they see no evidence that sacrifice, if required, will be shared equitably, and they have not been presented with any clear and compelling choices to make. Consequently, Americans stagger from price increase to price increase without any widespread shared agreement about what goals are to be pursued and what is to be done to achieve them. In the meantime, until the need to choose becomes clear, Americans will go on assuming that they can have economic well being *and* the quality-of-life values of more leisure and a clean environment *and* the enforcement of entitlements in the areas of health, work, safety, security, *and* the egalitarian rights of those slighted in the past.

If the old consensus still prevailed, that is, if the country wanted to pursue its economic goals singlemindedly without undue concern for other values, the diagnosis of failed political will might have made sense. But the diagnosis is less valid under today's conditions of dissensus and confusion. The notion of failed political will implies that the old consensus (a working agreement on the primacy of economic goals and how to achieve them) exists but that somehow we have failed to put it to work, much in the way that someone will say "I know I should quit smoking, but I just don't have the willpower to do it." But the old unwritten agreements of the past have broken down. They no longer inform and shape the policy making process. The chances are that they can be repaired or restored—to be sure, along new lines. But it is consensus rebuilding that is called for, not moral exhortation to pull up our socks and exercise our political will.

In what follows, I describe the series of shocks that in recent years have thrown the American public off balance; I then show how very different have been the responses of leadership groups and the public to these shocks; and finally, I try to demonstrate that the process of building consensus, while difficult, is not impossible. By the end of the chapter it should be clear why I believe that the "failure of political will" explanation points us in the wrong direction—away from, rather than toward, a strategy of effective action against the root causes of inflation.

The Shock Waves

As we emerge from the 1970s and enter the 1980s, I do not think it overstates the matter to recognize that the nation is reeling under the impact of a series of abrupt and large-scale changes occurring simultaneously in the economic, political, and cultural spheres. Any one of these changes would be enough to throw the country off balance momentarily, but, coming all together as they have, they have produced genuine disequilibrium, stress, anxiety, and confusion. There is no evidence that the American character has changed, but the national mood and outlook have shifted measurably. What we are now confronting is a serious problem in national adaptation to new conditions in the geopolitical/cultural environment.

The most familiar changes, those most readily documented and comprehended, are in the economic and geopolitical sphere. Our swelling trade deficits, growing under the increased costs of imported oil, are being matched by international uncertainty about the stability of the dollar and our dependence on the Moslem countries of the Middle East which, even before the Khomeini revolution in Iran, could hardly be counted as allies. Private sector productivity gains, averaging 3 percent in the postwar period, flattened out to near zero by 1980. And while disposable family income has increased by over 50 percent since 1972, the average price of a new single-family house has increased by over 100 percent in the same period, placing the "home of our own" feature of the American dream out of the reach of many of our citizens. The realities of an inflation-ridden economy have ballooned consumer debt and relentlessly escalated the cost of living.

Understandably, these changes in American economic conditions have been accompanied by drastic alterations in public morale, at least momentarily. Accustomed to steady growth in a world responsive to American influence, we have gone overnight from a nation of optimists to a nation of pessimists.

A study by Yankelovich, Skelly, and White found that in 1974, with a recession in full swing, only 23 percent of the American public admitted to being worried about paying for the rent or upkeep of their homes or apartments; in 1979, that figure doubled to 48 percent. In the same 1979 sampling, a whopping 62 percent agreed with the statement that "Americans should get used to the fact that our wealth is limited and that most of us are not likely to become better off than we are now."

Gallup surveys found that in 1971, only 30 percent of the public expressed dissatisfaction with the economic future facing them and their families. A majority of over 60 percent now voice that dissatisfaction. Traditional optimism toward the role played by technology has fluttered, and then reversed too. Yankelovich, Skelly, and White report in 1974, a 40 percent minority believed that "we are entering an era of enduring shortages, not just a lull before new technology gets us back to normal." By late 1978, those agreeing had become a 62 percent majority.

Perhaps the most telling and unsettling indicator of growing economic stress and pessimism is the response to the statement that "we are fast coming to a turning point in our history. The Land of Plenty is becoming the Land of Want." In 1979, 72 percent of Americans agreed with that grim assessment of the nation's prospects—and their own.

If the economic changes that have set the nation reeling are those most familiar to us, then the least familiar and perhaps the most subtle are the massive shifts taking place in the cultural domain, where changes in goals, values, and lifestyles have been reshaping the contours of American life. In family organization, long considered the bedrock of American normalcy, transformations have taken place at a nearly dizzying pace. Single-parent households, childless marriages, people living alone, and paternal custody rights have taken the unitary image of the American family and made it into a new mosaic of options—seemingly overnight. For example, in 1980 more than one out of four households in the United States consisted of a person living alone or with an unrelated person, a 66 percent increase since 1970 and a major alteration in what has long been considered the "traditional" family pattern. That pattern, enshrined in Norman Rockwell's vignettes, portrayed a full-time working father supporting a stay-at-home wife and one or more children. Three decades ago, that portrait accurately described more than 70 percent of American households; but today barely 15 percent fit the mold. And in the same period, the divorce rate has nearly doubled.

In the workplace, the very meaning of the word "job" has required redefinition. Formerly the province of a male breadwinner supporting a family, the labor market has seen successive waves of nontraditional workers enter the field. Two-thirds of all mothers are in the labor force now, including more than 40 percent of mothers of children under six years of age. In the period since 1970, there has been an increase of over 70 percent in the number of women rising to management positions.

In addition to changes wrought by redefined sex roles in the family and workplace, virtually every social sphere has been affected by expanded opportunities available to—and demanded by —women. For what must surely be the first time in human history, more American women are entering and populating institutions of higher education than men.

These changes are more than merely shifts in population or quirks of the marketplace; attitudes which define a national cultural orientation are also undergoing far-reaching changes. In a society which from its beginnings took pride in the self-denying work ethic of its people, more than 75 percent of Americans now reject the proposition that they should be willing to work at a boring job as long as the pay is adequate, and nearly 60 percent no longer believe that a man with a family is obligated to take a high-paying job over one that offers less money but is more personally satisfying (Yankelovich, Skelly, and White, 1978).

Although a majority of Americans still marry and raise families, the average age for marriage for both men and women has risen yearly in the past generation, and attitudes toward those who choose not to marry have changed dramatically. In the 1950s, when Americans were asked to describe what kind of person would choose to remain unmarried, 80 percent saw such an individual as either immoral, selfish, or neurotic. Today, barely 25 percent express any negative judgment at all toward the "single life," according to a study by the Institute for Social Research at the University of Michigan.

These geopolitical, economic, and cultural transformations have also been interpenetrated by changes occurring in the domestic political environment. After almost a half a century, the rise of what might be called the American liberal political orientation shows signs of breaking apart without providing indications of what might come next. The near unanimity of liberal political concern, which sustained the American version of the welfare state since the election of Franklin Roosevelt during the Great Depression, has motivated and funded massive assaults against poverty, illiteracy, ill health, and unequal opportunity. But ongoing support for the welfare state turns out to be more dependent on continued growth and economic well-being than many of its adherents had assumed. As long as a majority of Americans felt they themselves were making economic progress, they were willing to see the vulnerable, less fortunate members of the society receive a helping hand from the "common fund" of tax dollars. But an extended period of empathy and willingness to help others depends on people who do not feel themselves victimized by circumstances. When almost everyone feels deprived and hurting, beset by events beyond their control, the attitude becomes: "Help *us*; we're vulnerable too."

Of course, one of the central features of the liberal welfare state is administration by big government, and it is in the realm of attitudes toward government that the nation both generates and absorbs the shock of new circumstances. In recent years, disillusionment with government has spread rapidly, a fact well documented in studies going back to the 1950s. In 1958, only two out of five Americans (42 percent) suspected government of wasting our tax dollars; we have now reached a point where an unprecedented three out of four citizens (75 percent) feel that the government "wastes a lot of money we pay in taxes" (studies by the University of Michigan Center for Political Studies and CBS/New York *Times*).

In addition to wastefulness, there is the growing sentiment that the government is run by a few big interests for their own benefit, as opposed to being run for the benefit of all. Studies at the University of Michigan show that in 1964, a 28 percent minority subscribed to that view; the figure is now over 65 percent. Similarly, today only 29 percent of Americans feel that they can "trust the government in Washington to do what is right" most of the time, down from a 56 percent level of trust and confidence in the mid-1960s. And in an expression of growing alienation from those entrusted with the reins of government, more than 60 percent of the public now feels that the "people running the country don't really care" what happens to average people, a figure that was a 26 percent minority opinion as recently as 1966, according to Louis Harris Surveys.

Another cause of the breakdown of the liberal orientation is less often discussed because it is less often measured. It lies in the hidden incompatibility between some of the values which support the welfare state and those which characterize the majority of taxpaying Americans. For example, the welfare state tends to define fairness in terms of peoples' needs and rights, equating the two. If there is a need for education, medical care, or other social service, then it is assumed that one is entitled to it as a matter of legal right. By extension, if it is a right, then the government is bound and obligated to guarantee that it is provided. However, this conception of fairness often clashes with older, more traditional concepts of fairness based on the notion of deserving, the vehicles of which are hard work, effort, and dedication, rather than entitlement and need. Over the past few years, these clashes have surfaced more frequently. In troubled economic times, the American public, besieged by changes which often defy comprehension, has turned back to traditional values which are opposed to the ethic of the liberal welfare state. But in casting about for clarity in the midst of change, the American people are burdened with another problem: leadership groups too immobilized by ideology to offer leadership.

Three Visions of America

On the scale on which they have been occurring, these changes are not the sort that can be digested and adapted to overnight. An economy and a world role suddenly perceived as unstable; the emergence of new social values which redefine marriage and the family, transform the workplace and attitudes toward work itself;

a political orientation by which we have charted a national course for almost a half century suddenly called into question: these are unbalancing shocks, and a full understanding of how these changes have been absorbed and how their effects have been manifested is an indispensable starting point for any understanding of where we go from here.

Faced with these changes in our social, political, and economic environment, the American public and the American leadership have not reacted in the same, or even similar ways. Leadership in this case does not mean only or even primarily the President, members of Congress, or even politicians. Opinion leaders representing the broad array of people in significant positions in corporations, the media, financial institutions, universities, foundations, the arts and sciences, the church, and activist organizations, almost without exception have reacted differently to the features of our "new era" than the American public at large.

In reacting to the changes occurring around us, those in leadership circles have shown a tendency to respond ideologically rather than pragmatically. They have tended to align themselves along one of three distinct ideological paths, each of which leads to a substantially different "vision" of where the nation should direct its energies. These ideological cleavages have existed before, of course, but the urgency of our present economic, social, and political dilemmas has deepened them. To their most enthusiastic adherents, compromise with the other ideological positions is seen as a willful betrayal of *the* only possible moral and practical solution to our problems, rather than as a normal part of the political process.

THE INDUSTRIAL VISION

This perspective finds its strongest support in the upper echelons of the business and financial community, and in neoconservative "think tanks" such as the American Enterprise Institute, the Hoover and Hudson Institutes. It is represented by the *Wall Street Journal, U.S. News and World Report, Business Week, Forbes, Fortune, The Public Interest, Commentary,* and other media.

Those who hold the industrial vision strongly endorse economic growth, greater emphasis on capital formation, reinvestment in productive plant and technology, improved competitiveness abroad, and efforts to improve productivity. They see GNP growth as the most crucial measure of national progress and well-being. They are actively concerned with controlling rampant inflation and view inflation as a major enemy of the free-market system. Those who hold the industrial vision are deeply concerned with issues of cost-effectiveness, efficiency, and competitiveness, and thus perceive large-scale government regulation and spending as highly damaging. They endorse, and indeed promote, faith in science and technology. And they adhere to a strong belief in the values associated with the traditional work ethic: loyalty, hard work for the sake of doing a good job as well as earning economic rewards, achievement, risk, initiative, enterprise, getting what one deserves by dint of effort rather than entitlement, and self-denial in pursuit of long-term goals for oneself and one's family.

Preeminent in the outlook of those who hold the industrial vision is the moral imperative of preserving and protecting the private enterprise system. Toward that end, those in leadership positions who subscribe to its principles want less government regulation, which they see as shackling further growth and development and adding to inflationary costs. There is also strong advocacy in these quarters for balancing the federal budget, for market solutions rather than imposed measures to control wage and price spirals, and for tax incentives for business to increase research and development, expand imports, revive the infrastructure of industry, and gear up for the increased domestic production of energy, including nuclear power. Inevitably in these pursuits, less emphasis is given to environmental, health, and safety concerns, with the expectation that here, too, American technology and innovation, set to the problems, will arrive at acceptable solutions.

Those leaders who adhere to this vision of a reindustrialized America necessarily come into conflict with advocates of another ideologically coherent vision of America, the "egalitarian" vision.

THE EGALITARIAN VISION

The egalitarian perspective is held by those in leadership positions who continue to be faithful to the ideals and the operations of the welfare state approach to social progress, even though the appeal of that approach is losing ground in popular sentiment. Its views are nurtured in the academic community, in certain segments of the professions, among minority groups, civil rights and activist organizations, and in government civil service, especially at the federal level. Its partisans are concerned with an equitable redistribution of the wealth that the American society has produced. It defines social justice in terms of rights and entitlements rather than as requiring special efforts aimed at earning benefits. It places education, health care, and employment among those rights which governments are obligated to guarantee and insure.

Those leaders who hold the egalitarian ideal are not in principle opposed to further industrial growth any more than those favoring reindustrialization oppose equal justice and opportunity, but they are less concerned with the requirements of industrial development than with distributing the wealth that is made available for pursuit of social goals. They tend to be mistrustful of both corporate ideology and the market mechanism, suspecting both of being something more than callous to the goals of an equitable, egalitarian society. Egalitarians harbor a strong bias in favor of a planned economy, and extremists in this camp support an almost vengeful program of income redistribution and leveling. Among these latter egalitarian partisans, there is an image of historical and contemporary America as a land awash with prejudice and discrimination, where social mobility is but a cruel myth propagandized to the poor, and where hard work and motivation count for little in the face of the great corporate-industrial machine. For them, the moral imperatives of social justice come ahead of concerns about cost-effectiveness practicality, productivity, or even the ability of the society to provide the resources necessary for the society they envision.

For leaders of an egalitarian persuasion, there is no question but that wage and price controls are not only legitimate but necessary tools, that affirmative action programs are valid, up to and even including reverse discrimination, if necessary, to redress past bias. Proposition 13-style initiatives are seen as reactionary and dangerous social and political developments. Egalitarians will resist budget-balancing initiatives, especially when these contain the veiled intent of cutting back on social welfare programs, and oppose, often with vigor, the decontrol of any of the energy-related industries which would have the effect of raising prices and give more power and influence to those in the private sector who already, in their view, possess too much. Regulation of the market is a key watchword for egalitarians, for as Arthur Okun has stated in *Equality and Efficiency: The Big Tradeoff,* "The anatomy of the American economy contrasts sharply with the egalitarian structure of its polity."

If the egalitarian vision shares with the reindustrialists at least a tempered faith in the benefits of continued economic growth, both seem to stand at odds with the third major ideological vision of where America should place its future stock, the vision of a "quality-of-life" society.

THE QUALITY-OF-LIFE VISION

Those leaders who can be described as adherents to the quality-of-life vision include both environmentalists and people interested in quality-of-life issues in the domains of work, family life, nature, architecture, lifestyle, and personal self-expression. Quality-of-life adherents are heavily concentrated among the affluent (especially those in professional careers), in the media, and in academe.

More than the egalitarians, whose policy initiatives reflect some ambivalence on the subject, many quality-of-life partisans perceive steady upward motion of GNP growth as a palpable threat to the "liveability" of both the nation and the earth. They tend to be more concerned with curbing the abuses of industrial growth than with growth as a goal, per se. Their goal is to preserve what gains have accrued to the industrial society thus far, to fashion a low or moderate growth society from this point onward, and to "live better with less." For them, the "full, rich life," built on bases other than ever increasing material well-being, has earned its due, and material incentives, technological advances, and "nose to the grindstone" work habits have been replaced in large part with an emphasis on leisure, physical and psychological fitness, self-fulfillment, and a new, more respectful harmony with the biosphere. Sociologist Amitai Etzioni calls this an orientation toward the "fifty-five mile an hour society."

Quality-of-life proponents view America somewhat differently from the egalitarians. For them, we have been too materialistic for too long, too wedded to GNP growth, too quick to strip the environment of resources we cannot replace, and too addicted to the technological "quick fix" when damage is done. Their attitudes toward regulation often go beyond desires for mere market control mechanisms into the realm of disciplinary regulation and extensive "zero risk" prohibition of dangerous products. The moral imperative of those in the quality-of-life camp is as firm as either the industrialists or the egalitarians, and is not to be compromised: the preservation of the environment, both physical and psychic, is the highest priority, and takes precedence over such concerns as costs, trade-offs, equity of distribution, and timetables for growth and expansion.

The existence of these three distinct ideological perspectives is particularly significant at this juncture of our history because it is the conflict among them and contention among their strong-willed adherents that is one of the major obstacles to a coherent national commitment to combat inflation, reverse our energy dependence, and correct our trade imbalance. As should be clear from this brief sketch, the moral imperatives of the three perspectives are not the same, and quite often, gains made by any one of the visions are seen as taking place at the expense of the others; each group is willing to make sacrifices in the search for solutions to national problems, but these very sacrifices often poach on the moral purity of the other contending visions. Those who stress the need to industrialize are quite willing to give environmental concerns secondary consideration; the egalitarians are more than willing to sacrifice some of the unbridled freedom of the market system; and those stressing quality-of-life concerns are willing to sacrifice economic growth. The conflict among these perspectives is not the *cause* of inflation and our other economic woes, but it is one of the principal reasons we have been unable to agree on what to do about them.

With the growth in recent years of single-issue, veto-group politics, each of the three perspectives has developed and strengthened mechanisms for expressing its political point of view. Lobbying with considerable effectiveness, obstructing legislation, and punishing candidates offensive to their particular goals, these leadership groups have considerably restricted the amount of political maneuvering room available—often to the point where compromises seem impossible. Each group is determined to preserve and advance its own moral imperatives at the expense of the others, and the net result is an excess of political will bidding us to move in all directions at once and allowing us to move decisively in none.

The Public

Our current situation presents us with many surprises, and one of them is surely the striking contrast between opinion leader reaction and that of the general public. In two distinctly different ways, the public shows itself moving along a different path than that taken by opinion leaders.

The public's response is, first of all, decidedly unideological. The American public could not be successfully divided into the same three ideological categories that serve to identify active individuals in leadership positions. On the contrary, the public is ready to embrace the essential ingredients of all three ideological perspectives, hoping to achieve the best of all possible worlds. It would love to see high technology come to the rescue and devise new sources of energy, both in the form of more oil *and* solar power *and* coal *and* synthetic fuel *and* safe nuclear energy *and* conservation *and* any other development that might conceivably work. It does not want to reverse the clock regarding our concern for the environment, returning to smoggy air and polluted streams and rivers, but at the same time recognizes that there might be a need to extend timetables which seek the complete elimination of environmental damage and impurities and hazards. The American people would like to see the development of good public transportation systems and would use such systems widely if they were available. On the other hand, Americans would almost rather go hungry than give up the family car which, however, would certainly be used more judiciously if viable alternatives were available and the cost of gasoline high. Similarly, the public shrinks from the injustice of seeing people forced out of their homes to freeze in the winter, unable to pay the price of heating oil; it wants to see such people protected. Nor does the public want to see high prices artificially boosted by government taxes superimposed over OPEC price increases. At the same time, though with some resentment, the public will adjust to the ever clearer market signals on oil that indicate rising prices for a dwindling commodity.

Practical minded and hard pressed, the American public is eager to preserve some of the values embodied in all three perspectives, and is potentially more willing to compromise on trade-offs and timetables than is the more ideological leadership.

The other respect in which public reaction differs from that of opinion leaders relates to stress and the response to stress. The economic, cultural, and political changes described earlier create enormous stress and confusion to which those in leadership react one way, the general public another. In the period prior to the mid-1970s we had grown accustomed to a rising economy, a relatively low rate of inflation, a greater concern with managing demand rather than worrying about supply, world leadership in the economic and political sphere, leadership in the scientific/technical sphere, steady advances in productivity gains, a set of political "rules" geared to a rising economy, and a culture in which the family, role relations between the sexes, and the work ethic seemed fixed, permanent, and predictable.

Rapid changes in these conditions have had an unsettling effect on everyone. The country's leadership circles, charged with coming up with adaptive responses to these changes and solutions to the problems they create, do not, unfortunately, have ready solutions; they have barely sorted out the problems. Consequently, they fall back on ideology. Ideology may not be as useful as a sound, practical solution, but it is better than panic—at least it feels better. The public is not charged with the responsibility for coming up with the answers, and at the same time, it senses that its leaders do not have them either. So, in their initial reaction to so much change flooding over their lives so rapidly and unexpectedly, Americans have been thrown off balance.

Their response shows many of the characteristics associated with the reaction to sudden stress: it is full of signs of inconsistency, overreaction, anger, denial of reality, wishful thinking, and other transient symptoms of the stress response. In certain ways it reminds one of the early stages of what is called the "grief reaction." In the first phase of the grief reaction those who grieve for a loss manifest a series of symptoms that eventually disappears as the loss is taken in and assimilated. I do not think it an overstatement to suggest that in modifying their economic expectations downward as they are lashed by the expanding fury of inflation, Americans are experiencing a real sense of loss. If, for example, someone has lived and worked for years toward the goal of a financially secure retirement and then approaches the moment of his retirement only to find that his pension fund has gone bankrupt, we might expect to see signs of shock, anguish, and disbelief among his first responses. He is likely to be angry, depressed if not despairing, cynical, and fatalistic. A year later, he will probably have settled on some sort of revised plan of action, and even if he is living with lowered expectations, we expect to see him making the best of things—which he certainly was not doing in the first moments of his shock, when his initial reactions were erratic and unproductive.

Some of these same symptoms illustrate the first stages of reaction of the American public to new economic and social realities. There is overreaction to and exaggeration of the changes, as in the survey which found 72 percent agreeing with the statement that in the United States, "the land of plenty is rapidly becoming the land of want." Then there is also denial and reluctance to face reality as with the large numbers of people who still refuse to believe that we can ever *really* be subjected to a gas shortage. The conviction (expressed by 71 percent of respondents in a national 1979 poll) that trimming government waste will by itself enable the federal government to balance the budget, reduce taxes, and continue costly government programs, is nothing short of wishful thinking. By alternately assigning blame for gas lines to the President, the Congress, oil companies, the media, etc., the public is surely grasping for scapegoats. What is crucial to remember, however, is that these reactions are part of a *particular stage* in a sequence of reactions, and, as with the man confronted with shocking news of financial instability just when he expected a secure retirement, we must expect to see that more realistic and adaptive patterns of behavior will evolve once the first shocks wear off.

The Linkage to Inflation

It remains to show the link between this political climate and the inflation problem and to indicate how the consensus needed for effective action against inflation might be restored. Limitations of space preclude the systematic analysis needed to carry out these tasks adequately. But they can at least be suggested schematically.

The link between the political climate of opinion and the inflation problem is a fairly direct one. Paul Volcker has shown that one does not need a national consensus to institute a rigorous and clear-cut monetary policy—though we might need one to sustain it if unemployment rises and housing falls in an election year. But greater consensus than we now have is needed to deal with other aspects of inflation: for example, cutting back on the runaway cost elements of programs with large constituencies such as Medicaid and Medicare; reducing military waste; cutting back the growing indexation of pay and transfers to ever larger numbers of people, a process that builds inflation into the system; eliminating the pass-along costs to the public of government regulation; bringing wage increases into line with the modest levels of productivity gain; cutting back on the level of imports of OPEC oil, and demonstrating to those in a position to support the dollar that we have a coherent energy policy. These and other actions that attack the root causes of inflation are going to require a substantial body of agreement on strategy and tactics, both at the opinion leader and public levels.

A brief look at the energy problem, one of the keys to reducing inflation, shows one form of linkage. The energy issue lies, and will continue to lie, at the heart of our economic problems. Even at the most conservative estimates, the United States will have to absorb at least a 10 percent annual real increase in oil prices for the next several years. Wishfully assuming an import level held steady at 8.5 million barrels a day and an inflation rate of 8 percent (also considerably under current estimates), this country will be paying out more than 400 billion dollars to OPEC nations over the next five years. If this happens, it seems unlikely that we will regain our economic balance and dampen inflation; and yet it will certainly happen if we do not devise a strong economic policy which permits us to reduce our dependence on imported oil.

A nation confronted with such a problem and united in its purposes and values should be able to find a way to *decrease* its demands for imported oil over the next several years, not merely hold its imports steady. But we seem unable to forge a consensus that will allow us to proceed toward this crucial goal. Without a political consensus in the nation, Congress is unlikely to act except in a catch-up, makeshift manner; private corporations and financial institutions are unlikely to depart from their own narrowly defined interest; and labor, the media, and the general public are surely not about to cooperate with programs whose motivations they question and whose efficacy they doubt.

Of course, any such consensus will need to draw from and be sensitive to the concerns of all three perspectives described above, for each has legitimate contributions to make. Those who emphasize rebuilding and reindustrializing America must be heeded in their concern that we not confine ourselves to conservation and cutting back without also committing ourselves to effective development and production. Nor can we afford to disregard the argument that subsidized and controlled pricing of oil masks the true costs of energy from a consuming public and gives the market false and misleading signals. Distortions caused by artificially low American prices have in fact contributed to the seeming insolubility of the oil crisis.

Nor can we turn away from the compelling arguments made by those who advance the quality-of-life perspective. Surely, conservation must play a key role in any attempt to reduce our oil dependency, at least in the short run; and just as surely, we must direct more attention to the development of renewable resources and to the potentially endless resource of solar energy. Similarly, we cannot dismiss their concern that questions of safety and loss-by-theft in the nuclear field have not been given adequate attention, considering the extraordinary nature of the risks involved. Nor is it realistic to dismiss their contention that values beyond economic growth and material well-being have become integral to the lives of millions of Americans.

And from the egalitarian point of view, there is merit in the argument that we cannot simply ration gas and oil by price and let our poorest citizens bear the unconscionable consequences, especially in parts of the country lacking adequate public transportation facilities. Americans do not want to heap added punishment on those victims of the energy crunch who struggle in the best of times to heat their homes and feed their families.

With some give and take in the political arena, these central concerns of each perspective could probably be worked into a characteristically American compromise and consensus. Given effective leadership and good communications, the public would support any number of programs that balanced the need for sacrifice with realistic elements of conservation; production of new energy; provisions for health, safety, and environmental protection; and a concern for social justice. The requirements are difficult but not impossible, given the immense resources with which we have to work. But it would require leadership to suspend ideology and become more practical and specific. It is a real question whether our leadership groups, left to their own devices and divided as they are along ideological lines, will be capable of setting aside their own particular concerns in the interest of the kind of nonideological consensus the country so clearly needs at this time.

How then can we best accelerate the process of building the new consensus we need to bring us to agreement on an approach to energy and the other sources of inflation? We should not pin our hopes exclusively on leadership initiatives, and certainly not on those segments of American leadership groups that are locked in nearly religious warfare over the nonnegotiable principles of their ideological visions. Our real hope lies with working more directly with the public. The public is more clearly in a preconsensus mode than are national leadership groups.

Psychologically the public is almost ready to begin "working through" to a consensus. What is needed is a clear picture of the choices that lie ahead and a format in which sacrifices, if called for, can be distributed in a manner consistent with the value framework of the American people. For if sacrifices are indeed necessary, whether the cost is in altered patterns of economic advancement, the availability of housing, or the use of the family car, the public must have the opportunity to be persuaded that choices truly are necessary, and sacrifices equitable.

In a democracy the most effective form of persuasion is one in which the public becomes an inherent part of the decision making process. The case of the recent severe water shortage in northern California is instructive in this regard. By 1977, the San Francisco-Marin County region in northern California had suffered from a two-year drought which had all but exhausted the area's water reserves. No one doubted the authenticity of the shortage, and no one stood to gain by engineering a prolonged deprivation. When the severity of the drought became apparent, county officials proposed a ban on all nonessential uses of water, such as car washing and lawn sprinkling, and called for substantial water rate increases.

When the plan was criticized, both for its inequitable use of water rates and for the unenforceable nature of its prohibitions, its terms were revised so that individuals could determine for themselves how to use a sharply curtailed water allotment. Before the plan was implemented, the Marin County Water Director allowed a two-month grace period during which he met with government officials at all levels, citizen groups, and representatives of businesses which would be most seriously affected by a continued shortage. All administrative decisions were publicly announced and public participation was solicited. When the plan went into effect, it called for a 25 percent reduction in water consumption. During the drought, Marin residents cut their water use by a whopping 65 percent, and consumption rates have not yet returned to predrought levels.

What evoked this positive and cooperative response? How was sacrifice successfully solicited? "The people here cared about their community," the county water director said later. "The life of the community was at stake. Once I was able to communicate what the stakes were, people responded. They responded tremendously." The director of the Marin County Mental Health Center observed, "People didn't feel powerless. They were given choices. They could determine how they were going to live their lives within limits. People felt after a while that it was almost a relief to pitch in and help." As the success of the program became known, the *San Francisco Chronicle* editorialized that "the spirit of sacrifice, exemplified in Marin County, is apparently prevailing throughout the state."

In principle, the country has all of the institutions needed to repeat the Marin County experience on a larger scale in order to promote consensus: a free press, a wide diversity of media, citizens organized into an incredible number of national and local organizations, political parties, a Congress responsive to the wishes of the electorate, an educated public, a large and articulate intelligentsia capable of presenting and debating choices, etc.

If I am correct that the preconditions for consensus now exist among the general public, then with these institutions, it should not, in principle, prove extraordinarily difficult to take the next step to genuine consensus. Unfortunately, however, it is likely to prove extraordinarily difficult. Despite all of our institutions, some key elements are still missing. President Carter is a man whose engineering background leaves him ill-prepared for the peculiarities of communicating hard choices to the public. His inclination is to lay it out for the public—rationally, crisply, and in one single telling—and then to tick it off his list as a task completed, rather than as a task that has just begun. He resisted tying in an energy conservation effort with the Iran crisis, even though the American public is more readily moved to action by patriotism than by policies that appear to have the enrichment of the oil companies as their goal, or at least their result.

There are other missing elements as well. We have an abundance of "think tanks" to devise options and choices for the government, for the military, for industry, for science and technology. But what think tanks exist to spell out options and choices fairly and objectively for the *general public*? Astonishingly, there are virtually none, and those that do exist receive little recognition or support. When someone wishes to take an action that may prove injurious to the environment, an environmental impact statement must be prepared. But no one thinks to prepare a "public impact" statement for the choices we confront on inflation. And if they did, the networks would probably refuse to present it because it lacked entertainment value.

As a nation built on the principle of free and responsible citizenship, we are surprisingly unimaginative in devising mechanisms that incorporate the principles shown in the Marin County example, where citizens can learn what the choices are and can have a voice in deciding which choice makes the most sense to them. Instead we wait until a Proposition 13 mentality forces our hand: we exclude the public until it desperately settles for a blunderbuss mechanism to make its wishes felt.

In actuality, the task of building a national consensus is more straightforward than many of the other challenges the country confronts.

Americans know that none of the choices that lie before us is ideal. They also know what it is like to scale down expectations and make sacrifices; these are tasks performed in individual lives every day, and given the right circumstances can be expanded to consideration of national policy.

Yet no one in a leadership position has bothered to work out the real choices from the public's point of view, to spell out the options that lie before us in believable, realistic terms, with their consequences made explicit. In 1977, representatives of the coal industry and the environmental movement convened the National Coal Policy Project, which met under the joint chairmanship of an executive of Dow Chemical's energy division and a former president of the Sierra Club. Seeking common ground on such sticky issues as pollution, utilization, and pricing, the project claimed "80 percent agreement" at the conclusion of the first year of work, and proceeded to move ahead to study specific policy recommendations concerning coal-use policy.

In *Energy Future*, the report of the Energy Project of the Harvard Business School, coeditor Daniel Yergin enumerates a series of specific proposals around which public debate could focus and action crystalize: suggestions that the investment tax credits applied to conservation improvements in the 1978 National Energy Act be increased from 10 percent to 40 percent, a proposal that a self-extinguishing feature be built into any windfall profits tax so that revenues from oil sales be channeled at least in part to develop conservation and solar power projects, recommendations that more of the over 10,000 municipal building codes and all of the utility regulations in the nation be adapted to provide for solar construction. These energy-related proposals and many more like them concerning productivity and other issues need the best thinking of enlightened technical experts *and* the thought-through judgment of the American people.

In the end, there is no other path as promising as full public involvement for the solution of our energy, inflation, and other economic problems. In the end, if we are to mount a successful attack on the inflation/energy problem, the American people must come to feel that they know what the choices are: the real choices, not the contrived or engineered ones. And they must come to feel it soon. Only then can they set about the important task of working through those choices and arriving at the ones which make sense for them—and for the nation.

One of the forces currently acting most strongly against the best interest of the nation is the sense that the American zenith is in fact past, that we must somehow now settle for lowered expectations on terms that are dictated from without rather than from within. If this pervasive negativism is allowed to dominate our thoughts and actions, we risk falling into the trap of the self-fulfilling prophecy, bringing about that which we most fear.

If we shift our thinking away from the "failure of political will" framework into a "breakdown of political consensus" mode of thought, it will at least point us in the direction where we begin to think about practical solutions. We will stop thinking in terms of the decadence and deterioration of the American character or of the twilight of American influence. We will start thinking in terms of what our real choices are, how to get them on the public agenda so that Americans can struggle with them, and how to engage the public in the process of choice so that when ideology comes into play, as it inevitably must, the ideology of democracy has a chance to prevail over all the lesser varieties.

Albert T. Sommers

2

The Challenge of Inflation in the 1980s

The Complexity of the Inflation Issue

In the extended history of the behavior of the general price level in the United States and other similarly organized economies, a long, slow, wavelike movement is clearly visible. The developed world's price level subsided until about the beginning of this century; the level has been rising ever since. The same statistical record reveals extreme bursts of inflation clearly associated with wars, followed by equally sharp deflations in the immediate ensuing years. The U.S. experienced considerable inflation during World War II, but in the presence of the most powerful network of controls ever installed. The partial success of the controls in suppressing inflation during the war led to an inevitable delayed burst during decontrol in the immediate postwar years.

But after this delayed response to the suppressed inflation of

ALBERT T. SOMMERS *is senior vice president and chief economist of the Conference Board. He is a fellow of the National Association of Business Economists, a member of several economic and business associations, and an economic advisor to the Ford Foundation. He is chairman of the Price Advisory Committee to the Council on Wage Price Stability. Mr. Sommers has also written numerous articles on various economic issues.*

World War II, the price level in the United States, and among Western economies generally, did not experience a typical postwar decline. Instead, inflation progressed, at first slowly, through 1965, and then in an escalating trend over the next fifteen years. Even intermittent recessions do not appear to have broken the thrust of acceleration more than briefly; modern inflation appears to have roots deeper than can be reached by cyclical experience and different from those that fed the long wave.

In what might be referred to as the earliest postwar decade reasonably free of the consequences of the war itself, inflation in the United States proceeded at a rate of 2.5 percent. From 1965 to 1972, it accelerated to about 5.9 percent, and in the period from 1972 to 1980 the rate rose to 7.5 percent. By the commonest measures of price behavior, the U.S. and most of the Western world experienced inflation at or close to a double-digit level in 1979. The U.S. entered 1980 suffering a 15 percent inflation in its Consumer Price Index.

Simply on intellectual grounds, this experience cries out for explanation. But much more than intellectual interest is involved. Indeed, inflation has turned out to be the crucially vulnerable dimension of Western economic experience. In the United States, it is now universally viewed as an unmitigated evil demanding diagnosis, prescription, and cure.

Most economists, at some point in their careers, have debated whether we do not in fact make too much of the inflation issue; if all prices and all incomes and all capital values generally inflate together, are we not simply shrinking yardsticks, without substantial relative effects that should disturb us greatly? Are not the cures for inflation, all of which appear to be so painful, and all of which appear to threaten genuine damage to the real world apart from inflation, worse than the disease itself?

The experience of the past half-decade appears to have laid these questions permanently to rest. It may have been possible to view the mild inflation of the 1950s as of minimal importance not requiring medication—perhaps even as a gently favorable influence, encouraging evidence of a legitimate and compassionate ambition to use our immense resources nearly fully, nearly all the time, and to distribute the output widely and equitably.

But the inflation of the 1970s is something else again. The difference between the inflation rate experienced in the 1970s and the 2 percent average rate of the 1950s is not simply a matter of numbers; it is profoundly qualitative. At some point between the two experiences—a mountain of quantitative research has failed to identify the point with much assurance—inflation changes its character so dramatically as to require altogether different appraisal; even, one might have thought, a different name. The 1980 rate of inflation is simply not a gentle restorative; on the contrary, it is a violent aggravation of economic and social problems. At, let us say, 9 percent (simply to take a round number conservatively representing the 1980 rate) inflation engulfs the real world in a flood of expectational and anticipatory incentives that distort behavior and sap the strength of real activity. Investment decisions acquire complex new dimensions carrying incremental risk; incentives to save deteriorate; the inherently capricious distribution of the burden imposed by inflation intensifies the struggle for shares of output, while the search for parochial shelter from inflation accentuates the general rate. The "money illusion" that lies like a veil between nominal and real incomes thickens to the point where it is visible to all participants in the economic process. The illusion moves from gentle cajolery to a vicious incitement to partisan constituencies, whose proinflationary competition displaces the ordinary antiinflationary competition of the general marketplace. Finally, the political pressures posed by inflation induce a stream of institutional adjustments that are not necessarily desirable on other grounds, and that in themselves often accentuate the inflation. With respect to inflation, there is a crucial trade-off not just between wages and prices, but also between the inflation rate and the institutional changes resulting from efforts to accommodate to it.

There is no constituency for general inflation; poll after poll discloses inflation as an intensely felt and deeply resented burden. At anything like its 1980 rate, it is an unwanted outcome, a defeat for economic and social policy, an indication of grave distortion in the workings of the economic system, and a serious concern for the system's future. The control over inflation, the necessity of preventing any further acceleration in the rate, and the extreme desirability of installing a downward trend in the rate can fairly be described as among the principal economic challenges facing the country in the 1980s.

Managing the inflation rate back down again would seem to require a solid determination of the cause of inflation as a basis for treatment. There is, of course, an immense literature on inflation, ranging from the dangerously simplistic versions of partisan political debate all the way to the distinguished opacity of the professional journals. Almost all of the political rhetoric, and even some of the professional research, assumes that inflation results primarily, if not exclusively, from a single behavior pattern of the system; one result, one cause. At this moment, federal budget deficits, or years of accumulating budget deficits, are widely regarded as the principal cause of inflation, certainly among politicians, and now perhaps even among the public at large. Slightly more esoteric, but still widely held, is the view that excessive creation of money and credit is the essential cause. Inflation of wages, a consequence of union power, probably ranks as the third most popular individual cause. Excessive burdens of regulations, culminating in immense measures of the aggregate costs imposed on the system, and then perhaps our productivity failures (attributable to excessive taxation of investment and capital gains), and finally excessive profits earned by powerful corporations, would all score significantly in any poll.

It would be fortunate indeed if the causes of inflation could be narrowed down to one or a few simple processes or simple policies; then one or a few silver bullets would free us forever. Unhappily, the hope for such precise diagnosis and cure must be foregone. Inflation is the resultant of multiple streams of causalities. Even simple classification of the causes is difficult and misleading; they interact in infinitely complex ways. Many of the supposed "causes" are reflections of inflation as much as they are causes; some alternate between being cause and effect in periodic reversals of polarity that are as common in economics as they are in physics. And many of the "causes" are associated with other aspects of the economic system (for example, its growth rate or its perceived equity) with which policy must also be concerned.

The subjects that inevitably arise in any discussion of why we are experiencing inflation are so deeply rooted in the system's total performance, and so profoundly interwoven together, that their complete description is very nearly a description of the total system in which the inflation is generated. In abstraction, it may be possible to define a system whose price level would be stable in the absence of any one presumed cause of inflation—for example, "excessive" government spending or "excessive" creation of funds; in such a system, the removal of the cause would terminate the inflation. But this is not such a system; the endless formulation and reformulation in the professional economic journals of principles underlying even minor components of the system—almost always with a suspicious increase in the number of variables—testify to that. Its infinite complexity, its continuous technological and institutional change, its international connections, the indeterminacy of its human element, and the multiple economic and social criteria by which its performance is judged, make inflation an inherent, generic, systemic characteristic of its performance.

The United States and all other developed democratic economies contain a secular inflation bias. Inflation is not just painted on the real outcomes by mistaken policies; in some degree it is in the grain itself. In philosophical terms, it is essence as well as attribute. Its containment requires general therapy, not a doctrinal knife. Any argument that "inflation everywhere and at all times has been the consequence of . . ." reflects an abysmally ahistorical abstraction; the historical lacuna is not filled by superficial reference to the experience of the T'ang Dynasty or price behavior during the reign of Diocletian. Modern inflation is profoundly related to *modern* technology, *modern* humanism, and *modern* democracy; in fact, these are likely to qualify as "ultimate" causes much more convincingly than causes that can be more readily quantified and treated.

Inflation Mechanisms

As generic as inflation is, a great deal is known about individual parts of the inflation mechanism and the nature of their contribution to the process as a whole. These inflation mechanisms are reviewed briefly below, often with unavoidable cross references to other mechanisms with which they are intimately related as cause or effect. The classification system here is by no means in order of importance; it attempts to move from extraneous influences to systematic economic structure to the evolution of the economic system and thence to social considerations bearing on the inflation rate. Finally, a brief note is appended on the international transmission of inflation.

EXTRANEOUS INFLUENCES

During the 1970s, inflation in the United States, and in most of the West, has been subjected to several sudden accelerations that have little to do with systematic sources of inflation, but have often dominated the magnitude of the results. The oil explosion of 1973-74 produced violent acceleration of the rate of inflation throughout the West, almost without relationship to the prevailing rates of inflation and the status of macroeconomic policy in the affected countries. The experience was repeated in 1979. In almost the same years, but apparently unrelated, agricultural commodity prices experienced abnormally high rates of increase.

To explain these increases as systematic would require a very powerful model incorporating international political and meteorological variables. To factors requiring such enormous generalization of models, the word "accident" is characteristically applied, and for present purposes these developments might well be viewed as accidents. Nevertheless, a few observations about them would appear to be in order.

First, they have had dramatic impacts on the inflation rate in the United States, often very nearly equalling what might be measured as the inflation rate freed from their influence. These "accidents" typically affect raw materials in international trade; for oil and food, of course, the price elasticities are low across a wide range of prices, and in today's world the consequences are powerfully inflationary.

In the more distant past, these explosions in the prices of such commodities would have seriously deflated the markets for other goods and left general price levels little changed. In the periodic famines of preindustrial history, the food costs associated with staying alive often absorbed most of the national income. In modern societies, the consequences of such sudden surges in the prices of essentials tend to be spread throughout the system, to imbed themselves in the ongoing inflation rate, and to accelerate it. Indexation devices foster the transmission of a local inflationary impact to the system as a whole, while credit availability tends to sustain spending patterns even in the presence of sudden elevations in the price of necessities. The result is that the impacts on living standards are greatly reduced, the composition of real spending is more stable, and the inflation consequences far more lasting. Modern economic systems, now heavily indexed and equipped with credit reservoirs, tend to resonate to price shocks from outside, preserving the energy of the shock and distributing it throughout the price structure. What had been brief cyclical disasters in the price structure now work their way into the ongoing rate of inflation.

Finally, it can be questioned whether the term "accident" is appropriate even for food and energy explosions. A stream of accidents, one might think, would distribute the accidents neutrally with respect to any relevant criterion. But virtually all major accidents are now inflationary, and virtually none are deflationary. The world as a whole seems now to be living close to the limits of its current supply potential (perhaps beyond the limits, if depletion of exhaustible resources were to be taken into account); accidental appearance of deflationary excesses is now a rarity, and modern economic systems absorb them without deflation even when they occur.

MACROECONOMIC POLICIES: THE MANAGEMENT
OF AGGREGATE DEMAND

Apart from the obvious impacts of developments in energy and food, the principal public locus of concern over inflation lies in the functioning of governmental economic policy and its consequences. In the postwar world, the United States, along with virtually all the rest of the developed West, has employed fiscal and monetary policies in an effort to manage aggregate demand, to keep it close to but not in excess of available real supplies. In the course of this effort, it has generally run a federal budget deficit, and the accumulating financing of the deficits has yielded an almost steady, and now and then spectacular, rise in outstanding federal debt. The budget deficits and the rise in the outstanding debt are widely considered among most economists and businessmen as close to the center of the causality of inflation. And apart from the deficits themselves, the rapid rise in aggregate federal spending, measured in dollars, has been widely accused of inflationary consequences.

At least since the peak of the Vietnam War, a rise in federal expenditures has been principally a consequence of rapid extension of social outlay, in the form of Social Security benefits; benefits of other income security systems; and the cost of unemployment, welfare, training, and urban programs. These are relatively new forms of outlay, representative of the acceptance of new responsibilities by government in an age of democratic idealism and technological change. Actual expenditures on traditional governmental functions, and even defense expenditures themselves, have subsided notably both as a percentage of total governmental outlay and as a percentage of national output. Budgetary experience thus comprises several elements to which inflation can be related: the rise in spending, the change in the mix of spending, the excess of spending over receipts, and the cumulative financing requirements reflected in the rising aggregate debt outstanding. Perhaps the most common of all prescriptions for the reduction of inflation is thus to achieve and maintain a balanced federal budget—or, at a minimum, to achieve a balance under conditions of high employment.

But achieving a balanced budget has been a rarity over the past decade in the United States and in most similar economies. Indeed, the United States performance has been generally closer to balance than the experience of comparable economies; it is spectacularly better now than the Japanese and German experience. There are a number of reasons why budget deficits are incurred persistently, despite the widely held moralistic view that a balance is proper, and despite the announced dedication of politicians in campaign after campaign, throughout the postwar years, to achieve a balance.

A complicated social tide runs through the federal budget, propelled by a steady enlargement of the functions to which government addresses itself in response to the demands of the electorate. The spending side of the budget has been swollen by transfers to persons, in pursuit of the democratic objective of a more equal distribution of aggregate income, and transfers to state and local governments have been swollen by growing demands for the services performed by these governments, falling upon the heavy proportion of inflexible property taxes by which they finance themselves. The grants-in-aid to state and local governments, which in recent years have substantially exceeded in dollars the total federal deficit, in a sense provide those governments with access to the money-creating powers that reside in the Federal Reserve System and which are so readily available for the financing of federal deficits. Moreover, the elevation of tax rates to provide for the rising outlay of government is inherently limited by the impact of such taxes on private incentives and activity. In a very real sense, the deficits incurred by governments over the long term represent an uneasy and doubtless inflationary compromise between the pressing demands of evolving social systems on the one hand and the incentive requirements of the private sector on the other hand. Viewed this way, the deficits are revealed as essentially conciliatory responses to an inescapable conflict in the public and private purposes of modern economic systems. This conflict is described more fully below; but any description of the inflation problem that ignores it is naive in the extreme.

Moreover, it is not at all clear that the deficits are a *sufficient* condition of inflation, and the widely accepted public conclusion to that effect is not supported by much of the economics profession itself. There is no a priori reason why an incremental dollar of federal debt should be any more inflationary than an incremental dollar of personal or corporate debt. Indeed, private debt has grown many times faster than public debt over the postwar years and in most individual years, excluding only those in which recession produced a cyclical curtailment of private debt and a cyclical enhancement of the federal deficit. This circular inversion of the locus of debt formation during the short-term business cycle also appears to operate over much longer stretches of time; in the 1920s, private debt grew rapidly while public debt actually declined (in part because of statutory requirements for debt reduction). During the depressed 1930s, private debt grew slowly (in fact it fell sharply during the early years of the Depression) while public debt grew rapidly. During World War II, the volume of public debt was enormously enhanced by war financing, while private debt subsided both for reasons of credit control and because of the absence of goods to be bought by debt. At the end of World War II, federal debt accounted for about 65 percent of total debt; in the explosion of private debt that followed the end of the war, the public debt has fallen to about 18.5 percent of total debt. Aggregate debt of all kinds (personal, corporate, federal, and state and local) has risen about in line with nominal GNP—in fact, somewhat faster. In a sense, failure of private debt to grow rapidly is associated with conditions of general underemployment and growth of public debt; conversely, periods of high employment and of inflation are characterized by relatively rapid growth of private debt and slow growth of public debt.

As a last comment on the role of deficits and public debt in inflation, it should be noted that public debt formation is unlikely to be inflationary if it is financed by real saving in the private sector. The real saving may be achieved voluntarily, as it has been, for example, in West Germany, or the saving may be enforced upon the private sector by restrictive monetary policy that elevates interest rates and prices out private borrowers. (Unhappily, if the monetary constraint produces recession in the private sector, federal revenues fall, and the growth of public debt accelerates.) It is this question of where the saving comes from to meet the deficit that forms the juncture between fiscal policy and its deficit outcome on the one hand and monetary policies on the other hand. If real saving were to meet the investment (that is, the deficit) intentions of the government sector, the Federal Reserve System could be generally neutral; and, indeed, monetarists themselves agree that budget deficits unaccompanied by money creation are not a *sufficient* cause of inflation.

The monetary side of the dedication to sustained high employment has its own problems. The conventional and credible formulation of the relationship of monetary policy to inflation is simply that the more money and credit created per unit of real output —that is, the more money chasing each good—the higher, inevitably, the price level; and the proposition is generally supported by the long-term correlation of unit money supply (a standard measure of money, divided by a standard measure of output) and the behavior of the general price level. Even for this widely accepted nugget of monetary discussion, the case is somewhat more complex than the simple statement; in the most general case, it cannot be concluded a priori that if money creation were to be less, output would be unchanged. Only in the limiting case, when increases in output are controlled entirely by nonmonetary variables—that is, the availability of labor, materials, capital facilities—can it be argued that increments to many pass fully into increments to price.

Moreover, in the presence of an ongoing inflation attributable to other conditions in the system, the pressures entering into the formation of monetary policy intertwine with the business cycle in another way. As good as is the long-term correlation of money creation with the price level, just so good is the short-term correlation between the available supply of money, adjusted for inflation (that is, the real purchasing value of the measure of the money stock) with the business cycle itself. If recent history indicates anything, it provides reason for believing that an ongoing inflation rate has a formidable momentum, and monetary efforts to reduce it are, for a time, deflected to the real side of the system. Reductions in the rate of growth of the money stock to below the ongoing rate of inflation, leading to negative changes in the real value of the stock, are thus closely associated with the onset of general recession in the system. This carries the suggestion that the failure of the Federal Reserve System to validate an existing rate of inflation has nearly inevitable cyclical consequences. As the friction between social goals and private incentives sophisticates the application of fiscal restraint to inflation, so does the threatened decline in real money balances sophisticate the application of monetary policy. In both instances, the pursuit of sustained high employment in the presence of inflation produces a tendency for causalities to reverse; that is, for the inflation to dictate fiscal and monetary outcomes, rather than the other way round. In this sense, inflation arising from sources outside these general arms of policy tends to outflank and neutralize them and, on occasion, even to subvert them to its purposes.

These are the main obstacles to the direct and determined application of demand-management policies to an undesirable rate of inflation. But it should be added that a host of other complexities have made their appearance in the management of monetary policy, particularly in the past several years. The U.S. financial community has turned out to be incredibly innovative in its use of the resources made available by the Federal Reserve System. New institutions, such as the money market funds, and new devices, such as floating interest rates, have altered the meaning of the aggregates to which the Federal Reserve System links its policies, and they have altered the risk-reward curves affecting the decisions of lenders and borrowers in the light of any given level of interest rates. Inflationary expectations themselves have increasingly led the real world of borrower and lender to view interest rates in terms of their real rather than their nominal level, that is, by adjusting the rates for the ongoing level of inflation, and then taking account of the tax deductibility of interest costs. Perhaps even more importantly, the immense size of the Eurodollar market has produced potential and real flows into and out of the system that are under the Federal Reserve System's control in only very small degree, and has thereby reduced the effectiveness of policies aimed at domestic conditions.

A last component of the influence of monetary policy on inflation is institutional, structural, almost characterological; these are generalized aspects of the inflation problem in the United States that are discussed more fully below, but in their narrow application to monetary policy they tend to result in massive applications of credit in the direction of consumption in the United States. The U.S. financial system caters aggressively—perhaps more aggressively than any other system in the West—to credit for consumers. This is a heritage in some degree of the enormous historical growth and now the immense size of the domestic consumer market; it may also reflect certain investment-banking restrictions under which commercial banks operate in the United States, which may have contributed to their aggressive indulgence of consumer markets. In any event, the household sector in the United States is often the largest taker of credit in the capital market; recently, it has accounted for over 40 percent of all the credit taken down, and a very large share of the total credit extended arises from the commercial banking system. Some of the effects of this enormous application of credit to consumption are also discussed below; they are noted here simply as a strikingly visible characteristic of the allocation of funds in the market with which the Federal Reserve System must deal.

To summarize briefly on what is taken to be the conventional weaponry of policy in the management of the system and the control of its stability, growth, and price behavior, it would have to be concluded that the available powers, directed as they are toward multiple goals, can hardly exercise totally effective restraint over inflation originating from any other causes, and even over the inflation causes originating within their own areas.

The management of effective demand intended to achieve both high employment and price stability thus faces an awesome challenge. There is no abstract platonic "price" target to which such policies can direct themselves; prices are aspects of transactions of which there is a real side involving outputs, growth, employment, and living standards, and no certain measures assure us of the degree to which fiscal and monetary policies will distribute their influence as between price and output. The generalization that all stages of output can be divided into two categories—full-employment output and less-than-full-employment output—turns out to be a distinction with very limited usefulness; the range is a continuum, obviously, and rising cyclical output has been associated with strengthening markets and strengthening prices long before any contemporaneous definition of full employment has been satisfied.

This relationship is reasonably well expressed by the simple Phillips curve, which conceptually relates resource utilization to the inflation rate. Phillips curve analysis has been enormously sophisticated by research over the past two decades, in part by the entering of expectational variables with regard to inflation; that is, by recognition of gaps between actual and expected inflation and by distinctions between "rational" expectations and "adaptive" expectations. It is now often argued that while there may be a short-run Phillips curve of the typical shape, the long-run curve is actually vertical at a "natural unemployment rate" (set at about 6 percent by current analysis); that is, in the long run there is no real relationship between the unemployment rate and the inflation rate, and sustaining the unemployment rate below a "natural rate" is a temporary phenomenon achievable only by acceleration of inflation above expected rates.

Nevertheless, for practical purposes of analyzing the inflation problem confronting fiscal and monetary policy, the original relationship retains a revealing usefulness, and the history of the past twenty years suggests that institutional alterations in the structure of the U.S. economy have persistently elevated the curve as it appears on a chart. Relative to twenty years ago, any given level of unemployment is now associated with a higher level of inflation, and any given level of inflation is associated with higher unemployment. The location of the 1979 point on the Phillips curve, combining double-digit inflation with a 6 percent unemployment rate, was simply not on the Phillips curve of the 1950s. The general arms of economic policy must now deal with a system in which the inflation implications at all levels of resource use, and particularly at high employment, are substantially elevated. The conventional short-run Phillips curve now confronting fiscal and monetary policy no longer seems to pass through a politically acceptable combination of inflation and unemployment. It is a heroic assumption that all of this unfortunate elevation of the curve is attributable to the incitement of inflationary expectations by inappropriate policy—particularly heroic since expectations by their nature can hardly be measured accurately, and since, in any event, the expectations must have a footing in the realities of our inflation experience.

A consequence of the deteriorating trade-off between unemployment and inflation has been setting economic policy on a highly cyclical course over the past fifteen years, sliding the system up and down its Phillips curve in pursuit of a satisfactory resting place that no longer lies on the curve. American economic experience for the past fifteen years has accordingly been highly unstable—by rough statistical estimates, two or three times more unstable than in preceding decades.

The United States business cycle reached peaks in 1966, 1970, and in 1973 or 1974. Each of these peaks has been characterized by a progressively higher rate of inflation and, of course, the inevitable accompaniment of progressively higher interest rates. The recessions following the peaks of 1966, 1970, and 1974 have been progressively deeper, as measured by the unemployment rate and the federal budget deficit. In the last decade and a half, American economic experience suggests a perceptible widening and destabilization of cyclical fluctuation; the experience has been one of the great disappointments of macroeconomic policy, which in the first two postwar decades appeared to have achieved a progressive dampening of business cycle fluctuation. Indeed, if the minor cyclical experience of 1966-67 (it was so minor that it was never recorded in the business cycle annals maintained by the National Bureau of Economic Research) were to be attached to the cyclical record preceding it, it would have tended to confirm the widely held view that substantial progress had been made in taming business cycle fluctuations.

The application of full-employment economic policy incorporating a substantial role for the government budgetary position is by no means in itself an explanation of the inflation that ensued upon the successes of the early 1960s. However, in conjunction with other developments, including deterioration of the Phillips curve and the rapid escalation of federal outlays for social purposes, it committed the system to rapidly widening deficits under conditions of recession, and the reasoning implied abundantly easy monetary policy under these conditions in order to foster credit formation and recovery in the private sector. In the presence of an overriding commitment to high employment, recessions thus became, partly automatically and partly as a matter of discretionary fiscal and monetary policy, periods of powerfully stimulative policy responses, while the ensuing recoveries, in the presence of abundant credit, acquired increasingly inflationary characteristics. Inevitably, at some point in the recovery, as the unemployment rate subsided and the inflation rate rose, inflation finally displaced unemployment as the criterion of policy, and monetary restraints, increasingly severely exercised in each cycle, have ultimately been required to arrest the inflation. The history of the past fifteen years has thus been of increasingly powerful alternations of fiscal stimulus during recession and monetary restraint in the late stages of expansion. In a sense, the ordinary business cycle that is traceable far back into the nineteenth century has been increasingly energized by periodic alternations of stimulative and restrictive policies, all in search of a political resting place.

CONSUMPTION AND INVESTMENT

If the underlying conditions apart from manipulations of policy that enter into our inflationary experience had been less intense and if the system's Phillips curve had not been elevated by other alterations of the structure, the application of these policies might have had only moderate cyclical effects; but in the presence of many other reasons for the strengthening of inflation, it has produced a degree of cyclicality whose consequences were to reinforce the inflation rate itself. In each of the expansions of the past decade or so, consumption booms have made their appearance early and helped to drive the system toward full employment; as the inflation rate then rose, severe applications of monetary restraint acted to truncate the investment response to these consumption booms. The increasingly vigorous cycle imposed on the system by the alternations of policy have thus in effect tended to swell the consumption side of the system in a long-term sense, while shrinking the investment side. In some considerable degree, the inflation surrounding us today is an accumulating residue of this cyclical history; swollen consumption demands, fed by the abundant availability of credit in early stages of business recovery, now press heavily on an inadequate and aged physical stock whose growth has been periodically interrupted by soaring costs of capital at precisely the time when investment expectations would otherwise have been strong. In this sense, as well as in some other respects described below, the effort to purchase cyclical stability at high levels of employment has been dissipated in a secular elevation of the inflation rate. In one special form—other such forms will be found throughout this description of the sources of inflation—the point illustrates a proposition of wide generality; even inherently desirable efforts to reshape the outcomes that would be produced by a free market system almost always have a trade-off, and the trade-off is often inflation.

The impact on investment of efforts to manage the business cycle in the presence of a secular drift in the conventional Phillips curve is only one of several streams of history that have converged on the investment function and affected its contribution to cost-reducing productivity improvement. In the United States, preeminently among developed economies, the function of investment resides virtually totally in the private business sector, where it must compete with consumption for financial and real resources left after the preemptive actions of government. And the American capacity to consume is catered to perhaps more intensely than anywhere else in the world. The reasons for this involve historical and characterological issues peculiar to the United States that are described more fully below, but it should be noted here that consumption takes a considerably higher proportion of total output in the U.S. than in West Germany or Japan, for example, and evidently in most other developed systems. The institutional elements bearing on this partly regrettable performance include the enormous intensity of the marketing effort directed at the American consumer, who for so long provided American business with the world's largest domestic market. It includes financial institutions that behave far more aggressively in the extension of consumer credit than in most other countries. And it includes a degree of adversary relationship between the investing business sector and the government sector that is at least as difficult as in any other mixed economy and more difficult than in many.

Left alone and caught, in some degree, between the increasing demands of government in an age of social responsibility on the one hand and the consuming passion of a society inclined to measure its performance by conventional living standards on the other, investment has had a hard time in the United States—not by any means a fatal time, but a hard time. In response to the encroachments of consumption and government on the supply of resources available to investment, most other developed mixed economies moved decades ago toward public investment in productive facilities; United States tradition has up to now foreclosed this avenue to faster investment. Under these conditions, one might expect an offsetting solicitude for the investment function; but in many respects, whose importance is difficult to judge, the solicitude has been thin and undependable.

The general level of business taxes in the United States is still somewhat lower than in most other comparable economies, but it remains high by our own standards. And the tax treatment of recovery of investment capital through depreciation appears to be about the least favorable in the Western World. Taken together with the cyclical interruptions of investment described above and the intense competition for funds in a market so heavily participated in by the household sector, the investment function is simply in equivocal condition in the United States. While the actual share of output taken by investment does not appear to have deteriorated over time (in 1979, fixed business investment represented about as high a share of total output as in any postwar year), the general level of investment appears to have been inadequate to maintain the capital stock in a condition of vigorous growth and technological efficiency. The broadly recognized technological superiority and low real costs of American industry twenty years ago are now challenged and equalled by several other countries and, in several countries, evidently surpassed in a number of industries. The condition of the U.S. capital stock is doubtless one element in the bewildering productivity performance of the United States over the past decade, during which the rate of gain in aggregate efficiency of labor use has subsided by as much as a full percentage point. In 1979, productivity for the system as a whole was apparently negative—the third such experience in the past dozen years.

PRODUCTIVITY EXPERIENCE

The relationship between productivity gain and the course of inflation is not quite the simple mathematical link that is often assumed. With a given labor input, higher productivity inevitably yields higher output; and at any given wage level it means lower unit labor costs, which in turn are closely correlated with prices. But the givens in this simple model are quite important and cannot automatically be assumed to be fixed. Productivity and employment can be inversely related, at least over the short term (the experience of the last few years in the United States, in which job creation has accelerated as productivity has subsided, carries this suggestion); but even ignoring this relationship, arithmetic cannot assure that the enlargement of the total output pie is necessarily associated with a less intense competition for shares of the pie.

There is, nevertheless, a broadly held supposition that good productivity performance is antiinflationary and bad productivity performance proinflationary, and the supposition is warranted. It is obviously warranted in the very short term, where the high volatility of productivity performance is imposed upon an employee compensation level that is rising steadily, thus yielding sharp elevations in unit labor costs, as in 1974 and again in 1979. But it is warranted in a long-term sense as well. The productivity failures of the past dozen years surely have some general bearing on the persistent secular elevation of the inflation rate.

The attribution of the deterioration in U.S. productivity experience to its own multiple possible causes has itself turned out to be an immensely difficult task, and the results even after massive study remain highly uncertain. In one of the most recent and exhaustive of such studies, fully two-thirds of the decline in productivity in nonresidential business is attributed to an undifferentiated residual, and only an immaterially small fraction is attributed to changes in capital facilities per person employed. The minimal consequence attributable to change in the capital stock is surprising and almost certainly a consequence of the highly imperfect available knowledge on the size, age, and quality of the capital stock itself. Even conclusions produced by impeccable applications of mathematics must in the end pass the test of common sense; and it is only common sense to argue that American productivity experience would have been considerably better in the 1970s if investment had proceeded at a significantly higher rate.

A large number of other issues, many of them difficult or impossible to quantify, intrude upon this simple relationship of investment to productivity and unit costs. Intensified governmental controls in the area of pollution abatement and also in the area of worker safety and health, however desirable and necessary they may be, absorb capital in the production of life qualities that are not included in conventional measures of output. In the last half of the 1970s, about 5 percent of total capital outlay in manufacturing industries was mandated to environmental and worker safety purposes. The more intense cyclical fluctuations of the 1970s —particularly the last seven years of the decade—have doubtless cost us something in productivity. The demographics of the 1970s —the large influx of young workers into the labor force and the sharp acceleration of female participation rates—may have had a significant deleterious influence on the average inventory of skills per worker within the labor force. It may yet be (although this point is not documented to my knowledge anywhere) that declining educational standards and a shifting mix of educational content away from productive engineering and craft skills may account for some portion of the experience.

And it must not be forgotten that the United States labor force, accumulated by declining degree of skill, is characterized by a pronounced slope of efficiency, as the accumulation reaches into a disadvantaged and poorly educated minority component. Given this downward slope in efficiency for the accumulated labor force distribution, the United States may have an earlier and more clearly defined point, at which the bidding up of the price of skilled labor becomes an option preferable to the employment of new or untrained workers, than prevails in most other economies. Both Germany and Switzerland may have had such a pronounced slope at times when they were operating with large numbers of relatively unskilled "guest workers." These workers were disemployed during the middle 1970s and greatly shrunk in numbers. If job creation in the United States had proceeded at the German rate from 1973 to 1978, the U.S. unemployment rate would now be 20 percent. Much of what may appear to have been expensive efforts in Keynesian stimulation of the economy in those years was directed at this employment issue, and successfully so. But the very success implied falling productivity, rising unit labor costs, and accelerating inflation.

A POSTINDUSTRIAL MIX

A further element in appraisal of this productivity performance is the changing nature of the U.S. economy and the output it seeks. It is commonly said that the United States is now in a "postindustrial" phase of its economic history, in which the mix of output shifts steadily away from those sectors of the system in which productivity gain is most readily achieved and most readily measured. No one would wish to arrange the composition of American output solely to achieve a productivity target or, for that matter, an inflation target. Nevertheless, the increasing volume of certain kinds of service employment, relative to employment in goods industries where investment can readily elevate productivity, has necessary implications for productivity and for inflation as well. In the slow transition from an industrially-oriented society to a services-oriented society, the United States is said to be experiencing a structural compensation lag with inflationary implications; that is, its wage patterns continue to originate in the more unionized sector (and within that sector, in relatively old-line traditional "smokestack" industries) and spill over into a services sector of increasing relative importance, where the productivity gains are presumed to be inherently smaller.

This "postindustrial" argument on inflation deserves mention in any broad array of inflation causes, but it may be of limited significance; it may relate more to an inability to measure productivity in service industries than an inability to achieve it. Indeed, the basic distinction between service industry and goods industry has its uncertainties and data problems. The rapidly growing "business services" industry, one would think, may have productivity consequences in the goods industries it serves; it is hard to believe that the revolution in data management has not improved real productivity in financial institutions. And employment in many old-line service occupations is actually shrinking. It may yet be that in the 1980s it will be necessary to suspend the "postindustrial" argument altogether.

EXPECTATIONS

Interacting with all of these inflation-inducing structures within the system are the expectations of all of the participants—consumers, businesses, and governments themselves—with respect to the probable future course of prices. Naturally enough, the significance of price expectations, or expectations with respect to the general inflation rate, has grown more important as inflation itself has accelerated; and partly for this reason the academic attention to the significance of expectations has deepened and intensified over the past decade to the point where it has invaded many of the central propositions of economics and reshaped some of the thinking on which conventional stabilization policy rests.

Price expectations come in various sizes, shapes, and durations. There is the simple cyclical model of price expectations, involving their tendency to augment short-term demands, in order to beat expected price increases—a phenomenon familiar enough to purchasing agents, the buyers of capital goods, and now more recently, but very dramatically, the buyers of homes and big-ticket consumer goods. Under ordinary cyclical conditions, one would think that these price expectations would be self-fulfilling in the short term and then ultimately self-defeating, as the rise in prices weakens a market already partly exhausted by anticipatory buying. Price expectations of this variety seem to be an inevitable concomitant of free markets and even of the business cycle, and it is neither easy nor necessarily desirable to limit them. Even the wider and occasionally spectacular price movements to which they contribute, for example in commodity markets, are difficult if not impossible to control without measures so Draconian as to fundamentally alter the nature of the markets involved. Even in periods of rigid application of incomes policies, markets in which this natural short-term price fluctuation most flagrantly appears have been largely left alone.

But such relatively innocuous cyclical fluctuations in expectations have been dwarfed over the past decade by a more pronounced and recognizable uptrend in the general inflation rate affecting virtually all markets. Under these circumstances, and in modern institutional arrangements, expectations actually play a larger and no longer self-limiting role. It has been the tendency in the social and economic restructuring of modern economies (with their incorporation of "ethical" equity principles described below) to augment the natural feedbacks from price behavior to the income stream through mechanisms of the generic nature of indexation. Rising actual prices thus feed back into factor prices, elevating costs and thus tending to convert cyclical inflation into long-term inflation. At the same time, the price expectations aroused by actual inflation feed into product prices themselves, as well as into the factor prices. Prices, expectations, and costs are linked in a kind of squirrel cage, in which costs and price expectations race to catch up with prices and, in so doing, accelerate the rise in the prices themselves.

This squirrel cage behavior pattern tends to invoke the applications of incomes policies—efforts to get directly at the interplay of the wages, the prices, and the price expectations. And it is not only incomes policies that are involved; considerations of equity—not all of them unreasonable by any means—produce a stream of institutional responses to inflationary expectations that might be quite undesirable on other grounds and that often tend to exacerbate the inflation itself. Expectations thus play a role in converting what had been a largely cyclical phenomenon to what is now a largely secular phenomenon. In turn, the sense of secular inflation may develop finally into an ultimate response to inflation in a flight away from money toward tangibles. Elements of such a flight are now plainly recognizable in the prices of precious and other commodities, in real estate, and in the financial saving propensities of the system as a whole.

Inflationary expectations inevitably complicate the life of policy makers, particularly of the makers of monetary policy. Expectations and equity considerations come very close to compelling the supply of funds required to meet them; if the supply falls short, the rise in the price level to which the lagged effects of expectations stand as one of the principal causes may produce continuing inflation and a decline in the real value of money balances sufficient to produce recession. In recent cycles, inflation has continued, and even accelerated, into the early stages of recession induced by restrictive monetary policy and has thus seemed to compound the losses of output, saving, and investment. Expectations contribute to making inflation a durable opponent for monetary policy—far more durable than it appears in the simple aphorisms about the relationship of money to inflation.

In the light of the sense of accelerated inflation of the past decade, the relation of inflation to interest rates has also been a matter of substantial empirical study. The widespread awareness of inflation—the now clearly visible veil between real and money outcomes—has inevitably altered the interpretation of borrowing costs themselves; the calculation of "real interest rates," which used to be the province of the specialist, is now presumed to be the common knowledge of all, and all engage, intuitively if not professionally, in the business of subtracting the inflation rate from the prevailing interest rate to measure the real cost of money.

In financial markets, the distinction between real and nominal interest rates is ordinarily stated as conditioning the lender to demand a "real" return on his investment; in nonfinancial markets, inflation offers the prospect to the borrower that whatever he uses the money for will appreciate faster than his interest costs, particularly on an after tax basis. Thus for both borrower and lender, *expected* rates of inflation become a major element in their behavior.

How these expectations are formed, and their consequences, have produced a wholly new salient of economic theory that has come finally to attack much conventional wisdom about economic policy and the management of inflation. The traditional view of inflation expectations is that they lag behind the fact; that is, that they are adaptive interpretations of past history, a kind of smoothed response to the experience of the past year or several years in the actual perception of inflation itself. In arguments too complicated to be well represented here, "rational expectations theory" now argues that the ordinary Phillips curve referred to above is something of a mirage and that the relationships shown in the Phillips curve are attributable in the main to gaps between expected inflation and actual inflation. If this gap were to be removed—that is, if inflation expectations were to be based on correct and rational interpretations of actual policy so that they would not lag or err— the Phillips curve would be essentially vertical; that is, there would be no response at all on the part of the unemployment rate to fluctuations in the rate of inflation. Indeed, models that substitute actual inflation for recursive or adaptive measures of inflationary expectations drawn out of past experience provide a kind of weak statistical substantiation for this reasoning. If the reasoning is correct, then the unemployment rate can be held below some "natural unemployment rate" level only when the expected rate of inflation lags below actual outcomes; an unemployment rate better than the natural rate is thus really fooling people (presumably temporarily and inequitably) about the inflationary consequences of economic policy.

The "natural rate" of unemployment is not a function of discretionary economic policy but rather a frictional level dictated by imperfections and lags in labor market adjustment processes, including the costs of job search and information gathering as well as the structural characteristics of the labor market including, one would suppose, the massive alterations undertaken in that structure for essentially political and social reasons. The conditions dictating the natural unemployment rate include the characteristics of the labor force itself, the distribution of skills within the labor market, the lower general education and job orientation in the disadvantaged tail end of the labor supply, and the disincentives to work inherent in social and welfare programs. In this sense, the natural unemployment rate is an institutional and demographic feature of the system; in a world of totally rational inflation expectations, it would be the prevailing rate, and efforts to beat it would simply produce fully discounted inflation. What was described earlier as an upward drift in the conventional Phillips curve is, in the view of expectations theory, mainly a reflection of increasingly precise—increasingly "rational"—expectations of continuously rising inflation.

The significance of rational expectations theory in the current inflation experience of the United States is still uncertain. It is doubtless important, but stretching it to the point of arguing that it dismantles all stabilization policy seems extreme. At the least, it should be said that each experience with sharply rising inflation over the past fifteen years has left a spreading residue of inflation awareness, and for that reason it is both more difficult and more important to arrest inflation itself.

The serious complications produced by heightened inflation expectations, whether rational or adaptive, suggest that the U.S. statistics on the inflation rate require substantial review and improvement and less spectacular reporting by the media. At this writing, for example, the Consumer Price Index, which receives the lion's share of all numerical publicity about the inflation rate, appears to be grossly exaggerating the rate, relative both to the price index for personal consumption expenditures in the national accounts and the general price deflator that covers all output. Understanding of the inflation process in the United States at present would also benefit from a clear distinction between its imported and its indigenous component. It is altogether obvious that at the last peak of the inflation rate in 1974 and again in 1979, a preponderant portion of the inflation was imported, and another important component has been inevitable domestic reactions to the imported inflation—in, for example, mortgage interest rates. (Inflation of this type can hardly be rationally forecast.) And, of course, the unemployment rate itself, treated as a single number, masks a range of structural conditions for which applications of conventional policy may be ineffective and inflationary.

SOCIAL AND ETHICAL CONSIDERATIONS

A last component of our inflation experience over the past two decades must be described as institutional, structural, historical (in its broadest sense, including technological history), and even ethical. For several decades—beginning even before World War II—Western societies have been caught up in a tide of history that has imposed substantial ethical principles on the operations of economic systems. The origins of these ethical principles may be shrouded in ultimate philosophical mysteries, but the emerging democratic systems of the West have applied them unremittingly to their economic systems. In so doing they have vastly complicated the problems of inflation restraint and radically altered the underlying structure to which antiinflation policies are applied.

Ethical interventions into the marketplace have released a torrent of cost-push inflation throughout the democratic West. By the radical alteration and "humanization" of conditions in labor markets, by the imposition of politically validated full-employment commitments on top of "labor markets" that no longer at all resemble markets, by the widespread adoption of indexation of incomes to prices and prices to costs, and by the enormous growth of distributive social costs entering into each unit of output, the social developments of this century have greatly augmented the level and durability of inflation. In turn, this inflation, upstream from the economic system itself, has outflanked, neutralized, and subverted the traditional restraints on inflation provided by fiscal and monetary policy. It might be said that the Euclidian economic space described by conventional market economics has been subjected to a social warp by the pull of ethical principles. In the changed institutional structure that now confronts policy, reactions are simply different from what they were, and generally biased toward inflation. The behavioral differences are augmented by technological change and its effects on jobs, skills, markets, and political attitudes.

Neither labor markets nor most product markets can any longer be characterized as the auction markets on which conventional economic theory rests. "Fix-price" has replaced "flex-price" across much of the system; auction has been replaced by "career wages" and "customer markets"; marketing competition has displaced price competition. The absence of downward responses in wages and now in most prices has at least partly vacated the traditional view that in the presence of relatively stable monetary policy, increases in some costs and prices would be offset by reductions in other costs and prices and that *general* inflation could not occur. Imperfect markets are now the rule, not the exception, on both sides of the market, and both sides of the market confront each other equipped with at least some degree of market power. The sociological and technological trends that gave rise to this predicament are hard to quantify, and they do not find their way into the conventional modeling of the economic system; but to ignore them, as most doctrinal solutions to inflation ordinarily do, is to miss the most important lesson of the past twenty years. Market principles now coexist, in our institutional framework, with ethical principles which derive from the inevitable egalitarianism of democratic politics and are augmented by social responses to technology. The result is a struggle for income shares between business and labor—a conscious struggle between powerful parties over what conventional economics treated as a residual outcome dictated by purely market conditions.

The regulatory costs confronting the system, which are now receiving an immense amount of well-deserved attention, are part of this social and technological history. The anticompetitive effects of traditional regulation are now widely recognized, and in some areas they are actually being reduced. But the regulation of technological impacts—on the environment, on the workplace, on the ability of consumers to judge increasingly complex products—are all adding to economic costs at the same time that they produce their unquantifiable benefits.

In these new forms of regulation, as in the growth of legislative efforts to improve economic security and job security and to more nearly equalize the distribution of income and opportunity, modern societies seek a reduction in social and technological risk. What mixed economies all around the world have been seeking has been more security without less freedom, reduction of risk without reduction of reward, fine-tuning for high employment without the selective controls by which to tune. These are, of course, sets of trade-offs; the failure to rationalize the trade-offs—that is, the compromise of incentive, the unwillingness to legislate the necessary powers, and the failure to recognize the limits of resources—means that in the end inflation does the reconciliation for us. Difficult to appraise and quantify, the structural changes attributable to democracy and technology (and the legislative responses of the system to these trends) loom over the inflation problem in all Western democracies and multiply the difficulty of reaching noninflationary outcomes.

INTERNATIONAL COMPLICATIONS

A final set of issues bearing on the history of inflation in the United States in the past decade is the international environment. The issues here are complicated and, of course, partly beyond the control of U.S. economic policies. They therefore place limits on what can be achieved at home in the absence of a higher degree of international cooperation toward inflation restraint.

No developed country of the West is entirely independent in that broad range of commodities which trade internationally, including not only oil but agricultural food commodities and a long list of essential extractive products—and similarly with money. In the postwar years, and most particularly in the decade of the seventies, international financial arrangements have grown substantially freer and far more complex; the money and capital markets of individual nations now operate in an international context that has impaired, to some degree, the power to make policy for domestic purposes alone and has often imposed powerful international compulsions on the system.

The decline and destruction of the Bretton Woods gold exchange system at the end of the 1960s and in the early 1970s have dramatically altered, and in most dimensions narrowed, the options open to American economic policy. The devaluation of the dollar under floating rates doubtless contributed to inflation in the United States in the 1970s; certainly, it removed one of the reasons why the U.S. inflation rate could be expected to run below the European inflation rate, as it did throughout the 1950s and 1960s. It is now generally agreed that the standard view of international trade adjustment, which had suggested that devaluation would be followed by a contraction of imports and an export-led expansion, has turned out to be considerably less than descriptive. Specialists argue that the decline of the dollar in exchange markets has contributed one percentage point and perhaps two percentage points to the U.S. inflation rate, even apart from the special relationship of the dollar to world trade in oil.

At the same time, throughout much of the 1970s, some major

Western economies have been in hot pursuit of more vigorous domestic growth to restrain unemployment—and spectacularly so following the serious and deep world-wide recession of 1974-75. For this reason and also because some of our major competitors have sought to stabilize the dollar through central bank purchase, using their own currencies, the global growth of money and credit has been dramatic—more dramatic, in percentage terms, than the growth of the U.S. money supply itself. A prevailing awareness among sophisticated participants in international finance that money has grown rapidly almost throughout the world has contributed in some degree to a flight from all currencies, which in turn has led to accelerated increases in the cost of many raw materials that enter into the U.S. basic price level.

In an environment of threatened or actual stagflation, employment conditions, as well as profitability considerations, often conspire toward protectionism in all Western countries, vitiating the advantages of international specialization and adding to the real costs of all.

There is thus a substantial international component to American inflation experience in the 1970s, which can be expected to respond only to international efforts at control. One of the arguments advanced for floating rates a dozen years ago was that they would free individual countries to pursue their own discretionary policies, relieved of the requirement to maintain their currencies at fixed relationships with any other currencies. But all Western democracies face the inflation dilemma described here for the United States, and each has sought, within its own political context, economic solutions that are politically viable. Relatively strong countries with relatively strong governments and relatively homogeneous populations have managed to achieve conservative policies in this situation. In Switzerland and Germany, the two obvious illustrations, at least monetary policy has been more restrictive than in the rest of the West; the growth and employment problems imposed by such policies have been absorbed in part by releasing the so-called "guest workers." In other countries in other situations (and the United States is one of these) the search for growth has proceeded unabated. In the United States, 1979 employment was 12 percent above its level in 1973; but the current search for growth has doubtless contributed to an inflation record less satisfactory than that achieved by West Germany and Switzerland, and the difference has been amplified by reactions in the currency markets.

Summary and Conclusions

No effort to explain the multiple interconnections that collectively constitute the "cause" of modern inflation can hope to be complete. Modern inflation is rooted not only in a social, political, technological, and ethical history, but also in the frictions that arise at critical interfaces within the system—the interface between government and the private sector, where private efficiencies confront public values; the interface between labor and management, where shares of income are determined; and the interface between the interests of the United States and the interests of other nations and groups of nations with which we deal. Most generally of all, modern Western inflation reflects a distribution of political power that is substantially more egalitarian than the natural distribution of economic power in a free-market system. Our political system is democratic and distributive, motivated by considerations of presumed social justice; our economic system is generally meritocratic and cumulative, motivated by self-interest. If there is a genuine historical challenge for the United States in the remainder of this century, it is to reconcile these differences in ways that preserve growth and constrain inflation within tolerable bounds. The challenge will occupy many future administrations. There is no way of going back to the pure market conditions under which, theory says, the causalities run directly and irreversibly from fiscal and monetary outcomes to the inflation rate, and general secular inflation is just mistakes. Nor is there any way of going forward in a single leap to a world in which ethical and market considerations have been fully reconciled and their inflationary frictions removed.

The implication of this description is that there are no one-shot cures for inflation, no simple remedy or combination of remedies. Antiinflation proposals that focus exclusively on balancing the federal budget, containing the growth of money, eliminating regulation, removing excessive profits, or reducing the power of unions ignore the systemic character of inflation and its deep roots in social history. To focus on any one facet of the complex responsible for inflation is to require a violent, narrow response sufficient to obliterate the other causes. Such a response is improbable, almost surely undesirable, and in the end self-defeating. But there are a number of broad principles to which national economic policy should adhere in its efforts to control deeply rooted inflation with minimal disturbance to the other natural objectives of public policy. With respect to these principles, specific applications are not hard to find, and some are raised here; but the difference between one specific measure and another is not likely to be great. It is adherence to the principles that counts.

PRELIMINARY CONSIDERATIONS

It has become customary to distinguish an ongoing or underlying inflation rate from the total inflation rate, the distinction focusing on such temporary or extraneous abnormalities as energy costs, food inflation attributable to noneconomic considerations, or the effects of higher interest rates (themselves a reaction to inflation) on price indexes. The distinction is useful in that it has a potentially high educational content.

It is also useful to recognize a related distinction between imported inflation and indigenous inflation. The statistical difficulties in disentangling the two are certainly formidable, but if the effort is to reduce inflation, it is vitally important to know what part of the problem lies beyond our immediate control, and the recognition should help to subdue the intensity of the struggle for shares that goes on at the interfaces. It should also help to sophisticate and clarify the responsibilities, and where they lie, for the management of the aggregate inflation problem. A wage-price spiral does nothing to reduce the aggregate burden of imported inflation, and it may well accentuate it.

The underlying domestic rate itself—which is now generally considered to be perhaps 8 percent—might be further distinguished into an inevitable, structural, and inherent component on the one hand, and a component for which our current behavior is responsible. The inherent inflation rate (it is tempting to refer to it as a "natural inflation rate," related to the "natural unemployment rate") is a frictional inflation, a heat loss, generated at the interface between ethical and market arrangements. A round estimate for the inherent inflation rate in the U.S. system today might put it between 3 and 4 percent, and the task for antiinflationary policy is to reduce the present underlying rate to this inherent rate.

In the containment of inflation, there remains ample room for discretionary macroeconomic policy. Rational expectations theory and its corollary in the natural unemployment rate do not relieve macroeconomics of a responsibility for seeking policies conducive to high employment while avoiding an independent contribution to inflation. At the same time, the natural unemployment rate thesis invites attention to the detailed structure of labor market institutions and the character of the labor force itself, which are presumed to determine the rate. These propositions are consistent with substantial efforts to improve those dimensions of the system, with a view to a reduction of the policy stimulus required to achieve any given unemployment target, and hence a reduction in the inflation implications of any unemployment target. The description here thus suggests a continued role for both macropolicy and targeted efforts at the unemployment rate. It does not suggest an abandonment of efforts at a joint unemployment-inflation objective, and it does not prescribe a sustained high level of unemployment as a "cure" for inflation.

Finally, the description attributes some portion of inflation to inappropriate institutional responses to inflation itself and some portion to an absence of evolution of our economic institutions, in the presence of considerable evolution of our social objectives and technological character. The description thus calls for an unfreezing of our institutional structure to permit pragmatic innovation.

Such innovations should disturb market competition as little as possible; effective markets are still the first line of defense against inflation and a principal source of the energy for growth and efficiency. Innovation is needed mainly where our present structure inhibits markets, urges them on to inflationary behavior, or where markets themselves have deteriorated, or where nonmarket, ethical objectives compel nonmarket methods.

RESTRAINT ON CONSUMPTION

Under our present institutional arrangements, the United States simply consumes excessively and saves inadequately. Why this should be so is a ponderous question involving inflation itself and the expectations for future inflation, the institutional structures that cater to consumption in the United States, and perhaps also deeply historical and characterological aspects of the system and its citizenry. However complicated and profound the causes, a number of devices are available for constraining consumption and improving the saving rate. They include, in the first instance, higher rewards for saving in the form of interest rates free of regulatory limitations and the reduction of taxation on both interest and dividend income.

In any discussion of inflation, it is a flagrant oversight to fail to note that for much of the 1970s, the household sector has taken down more credit in U.S. financial markets than the business sector itself. The international comparisons of the personal saving rate in the United States with rates in other developed countries are probably badly flawed; it is doubtful that the differences are as wide as they appear. But the consumption share in output and in credit markets is obviously far higher in the United States than elsewhere; the comparisons point to a characteristic vulnerability of the U.S. business system, both to the business cycle and to cyclical waves of inflation.

Flexible constraints on short-term credit extension for consumption, affecting down payments and length of term, could play an important role in restraining the percentage of output taken off the market by consumption, and they might well reduce the volatility of our cyclical experience. The much debated value-added tax deserves consideration for the same purpose; its large potential yield bears on consumption, not on income, and might well permit considerable reductions in tax rates that bear on income and saving. The prolonged downtrend in the personal saving rate in the 1970s suggests a widespread "underground economy" whose income is not recorded but whose spending appears in consumption data. A value-added tax would at least recoup a part of the avoided income taxes. And its yield could be used to contain the growth of taxes levied on incomes and payrolls.

INCREASING INVESTMENT

The United States is underinvesting, almost throughout the range of activities included in a broad definition of the term. Where the statistical information does not confirm this conclusion, it is almost certainly wiser to question the statistics than the conclusion. The fact is that however the investment rate may compare with output over the past decade and however this relationship has developed over the postwar years, the investment rate of the 1970s was insufficient even to maintain the capital stock, much less to enlarge and deepen it. This unpleasant conclusion bears on the stock of fixed private capital on which growth and productivity partly depend; it also applies to the housing stock, to the stock of defense equipment, and to the stock of public capital—the infrastructure of public facilities on which the private sector rests and which makes its own important contribution to total productivity.

In part, this underinvestment is a mirror image of overconsumption and undersaving. In the private sector, virtually every major American industry—the exceptions are new, fast-growing absorbers of new technology—features an age-distribution of capital facilities that bespeaks inadequate modernization and replacement outlays and hence steeply rising unit curves.

It may be that this condition is attributable in part to managerial failures, such as excessive concentration on short-term results and an absorption with marketing effort as distinguished from long-term technical competition, basic research, and product design. (It is not inconceivable that the incentives motivating senior business executives are concentrated in the short term, as is so often said of politicians.) It may reflect our antitrust laws, which inhibit concentration even where only concentration can generate the size of unit required for advanced technology and often conduce to the preservation of old, insufficient capital. It may reflect the impact of capital gains taxation on the returns to venture capital.

In any event, private investment needs substantial encouragement in the 1980s if the capital stock is to be rebuilt and extended. A simple and direct way of assuring an acceleration in the replacement of outmoded facilities is to accelerate the rate at which capital investment costs are recovered. A substantial improvement in depreciation flow would not only improve cash flows, but also would improve the attractiveness of investment in new facilities, relative to the continued operation of old facilities already written off. Its benefits would run more heavily to capital-intensive industries than to others, but this is precisely its purpose. No other device holds more promise for flattening the unit cost curves of most industries across their entire range, particularly in the range near high employment of resources. Dozens of other tax measures to improve the investment environment—affecting the treatment of research and development, tax credits for investment, the consolidation of corporate and personal taxes, the reduction of tax brackets affecting "unearned income," to name a few—have been proposed and many have been studied. Depreciation reform offers the clearest case and has the best probability of being legislated, but it should not foreclose other approaches.

IMPROVING THE SKILLS OF THE LABOR FORCE

The U.S. labor force is the other great input into economic activity. Like our capital stock, it is characterized by rapidly rising unit labor costs and deteriorating efficiency in the segment of the curve approaching high resource utilization. As with its capital stock, the U.S. labor force is unsurpassed over perhaps 70 or 80 percent of its utilization rate; thereafter, it descends in quality, educational attainment, learning ability, and job orientation perhaps more steeply than in any other developed country. The improvement of productivity in the United States at high levels of resource utilization depends as much upon improvement of the human resources available as it does on the capital resources.

The 1970s witnessed a long, expensive, and often exasperating learning experience in what works and what does not work in this crucial socioeconomic area. The efforts of the 1980s should be no less intense, but we can hope that experience will lead them to be more practical, more coherently related to each other, more sociologically aware, and therefore somewhat more successful. The obverse of this necessitous case for targeted programs aimed at the job skills of the disadvantaged segment of the labor force is that macroeconomic policy simply will not do this job. On this conclusion, all doctrinal economists—Keynesians, pre-Keynesians, monetarists, rational expectations theorists—seem in agreement. The costs incurred in this pursuit are part of the "natural inflation rate"; they are aimed at containing or reducing the "natural unemployment rate."

This in turn suggests that the guidance provided to macroeconomic policy by crude measures of the unemployment rate can be dangerously misleading to policy. One of the lessons of the 1970s should be the urgent need to remove work disincentives, particularly in the marginal tax rates applicable to the earned income of aid recipients.

FISCAL AND MONETARY POLICIES

The ordinary criteria for the behavior of macroeconomic policy are the size of the budget deficit, the share of government in the total economy, and the rate of growth of money aggregates. There are, by overwhelming consensus, budget deficits of a size and money growth of a rate that have plainly inflationary consequences. At the other extreme, there are policies in both areas that would plainly suppress growth, including growth in the quality of the capital and human inputs on which future economic performance depends. Macroeconomic policy should stay well within these extremes. (It is possible, but not popular, to argue that to the extent the U.S. context has permitted, it *has* stayed within these extremes.) In so doing, it will avoid being an independent cause of inflation, but it will still inevitably transmit some of the inflation originating in other parts of the system.

What is crucially important for government in the control of inflation in the 1980s is what it does, how it does it, why it runs a deficit if it runs one, and where the money goes that it creates. In this context, a large number of propositions are available. With respect to the spending and revenues of the federal government, it would be wise to accept a reduction of revenues resulting from substantial improvement in business depreciation. It would be wise to accept an increasing volume of spending for the public infrastructure. It would be wise to accept increasing outlays in the effort to improve the quality of the labor force, at the margin.

To fail to accept these revenue losses and spending increases would be to fight inflation in the short term, but to lose the war in the long term.

These influences working to enlarge the budget deficit can be largely offset by increasing taxation of consumption, by vigorous restraint over transfer programs that augment consumption and inhibit incentive, and in part by the curtailment of old programs and the rejection of proposed new programs. This applies particularly to programs that cater to local interests, particularly in defiance of market mechanisms, but it may even apply to ethically mandated powers that must be considered luxuries until the basic stock of efficient capital and human resources is in a clearly improving trend. In particular, government should avoid the installation of any new resonating devices by which inflation from any source is transmitted through the system; this includes all forms of indexation (with the exception of income indexation for retirees) and third-party payment systems lacking coinsurance, which amount to instantaneous indexation of a particularly uncontrollable kind.

These proposals do not by any means dictate where the federal budget should come out, and they do not by any means prescribe a balanced budget as the ultimate criterion of fiscal policy. Instead, they place upon the government a principal responsibility for the control of inflation through assuring vigorous growth in the efficiency of the private sector and its capacity to invest toward a more productive future. Budget deficits incurred in the effective pursuit of this objective are a contribution to the long-run control of inflation.

Similarly, monetary policy, one can hope, will avoid rates of increase in money and credit that would themselves be direct causal incitements to inflation. It is not clear that its present powers, which bear almost totally on the supply side, are capable of doing this efficiently; other devices that reach borrowers and lenders more immediately deserve consideration. But in its general functioning within the complex system of causes that yield inflation in the end, its principal effort should be to assure continuing availability of credit for investment and constraint on the uses of credit for other purposes. Frequent pronounced elevations of the cost of capital appear to have played an important role in slowing growth and improvement of the capital stock during the 1970s; feeding consumption booms and then starving the ensuing investment demands are a perversion of the function of capital markets. Where the money goes *is* important. In today's complicated and skewed markets—skewed by social forces, by technology, by the imposition of ethical standards on economic performance—the financial market can use some assistance and guidance in the direction of credit into productive use. Here too it is not clear that the Federal Reserve System's present powers, in a U.S. context, can achieve this outcome; its powers need augmentation if it is to operate in a truly long-term antiinflationary way.

In different ways in different countries, most of the rest of the world has achieved a more useful alliance between governments, central banks, and the private sector to assure abundant flows into investment; that is, they are more advanced in the reconciliation of the pressure for consumption that originates in mixed economies with the needs for growth of capital. In some countries, the result is achieved in part by tax structure and by deliberate restraint on the use of credit in consumption; in other countries, a partnership in the provision of the capital, including joint business-government ventures, credit guarantees, and even grants of developmental capital have been used to reach investment targets. This will require some relaxation of traditional American attitudes in the relationship of business to government—in the end, a relaxation is inevitable. Among other things, inflation is a symptom of a failing production system—of mounting pressures of demand on an unresponsive supply. A principal charge to government in the 1980s in its pursuit of more stable prices should be the invigoration of the supply side of the U.S. business system.

INCOMES POLICIES

An incomes policy is a tough, exasperating, unattractive, expensive alternative to the superb efficiencies of *ideal* free markets. But a large proportion of *real* markets—for products or for labor—no longer resemble the economic ideal. Nominal wages and nominal prices no longer respond to pure market conditions alone, and in general they do not decline at all. Only inflation can any longer induce downward flexibility in real wages (as it did in 1979) and in relative prices; in a sense, this is one reason why inflation happens. Technology and institutional change have delivered power to both sides of U.S. markets; cost-push inflation is evidence of the power, and the power is not accompanied by a commensurate accountability. Fiscal and monetary policy cannot reduce the power or install the accountability. This is a genuine inflation dilemma of modern democratic economies.

What to do about it? To install accountability, incomes policies have been tried again and again, in the United States and almost all European economies; the record is mixed—not great, but not as bad as the prevailing opinion. Incomes policies are an ethical response (setting "fair" and "just" prices and wages) to ethical objectives and market imperfections. More injection of ethical principles into the system elevates the odds that incomes policies will be more widely and frequently used. At present, they have proven to be a useful *temporary* expedient in containing wage-price interactions, but their general, permanent application would mark a further decisive departure from market economics. The cost is so high as to suggest rather serious appraisal of alternatives. A willingness to accept some inflation—the inherent rate—would reduce the intensity of this issue and bring it within range of more moderate and general proposals. A candidate for consideration is a statute modeled on our antitrust statutes, directed at "abuse of market power." The statute might convey investigative, deferral, and rollback powers and access to the judicial system. Such a statute would achieve a general accountability, at little cost to market functioning. No detailed regulation of wages or prices would be required, and no new reporting burden; but there would be substantial procedural and litigation costs in individual cases. The statute would confront a real and growing issue; without it, the high-employment commitment of recent legislation is really a nonevent.

Compulsory arbitration is a form of incomes policy; so is a policy of specific relaxations of antitrust restraints in individual industries for a transitional period, in return for commitments on price or rate of return. More experimentation in such areas is certainly warranted. Antitrust policy may reduce the intensity of need for incomes policies in one other important way. Interindustry competition remains powerfully effective and tends to offset the loss of vigor of price competition within industries. Horizontal integration among competing industries often produces little social gain in efficiency, and tends to vitiate interindustry competition; where this is the case, it should be resisted, regardless of considerations of market share.

Such a plan would represent a functioning of the social compact on which democracy ultimately rests. Inflation control is part of an awesomely broad array of issues. There is no real escape from this complexity. Efforts to treat the part rather than the whole, and doctrinal focus on ideologically heated parts of the problem, distract attention from the complicated reality. Conversely, treating the whole should result in improvement in many other aspects of the system's performance—its growth rate, the rate of job creation, its productivity, its investment rate, its cyclical stability, and, as a consequence of all of these, its political stability.

Otto Eckstein

3

Choices for the 1980s:

Core Inflation, Productivity, Capital Supply,
and Demand Management

Progress has slowed in the American economy since 1967. The growth of real GNP, which had averaged 3.9 percent for 1947-67, has been only 3 percent since then. Average unemployment grew from an average of 4.8 to 5.7 percent for the two periods. The rate of inflation, as measured by the GNP deflator, accelerated from an average of 2.3 to 6.4 percent, and was running near 9 percent as the 1970s ended. Industrial production showed a major retardation between these two periods, fading from 4.8 to 3.6 percent.

OTTO ECKSTEIN *is president of Data Resources, Inc., the country's largest economic forecasting and consulting firm, and Paul M. Warburg Professor of Economics at Harvard University. A past member of several government commissions, including the President's Council of Economic Advisors under Lyndon Johnson, he is also a member of* Time *Magazine's board of economists. Dr. Eckstein has written widely on economic matters, including* The Great Recession. *The author acknowledges the contributions made in the preparation of this chapter by Robin Siegel, Frank Cooper, and Diana Rigoli.*

Productivity dropped far below its historical performance. Its century-old trend of about 2 percent was surpassed in the early postwar period under the benefit of making up lost ground from the Depression and the war and from the extraordinarily strong U.S. international position of the 1940s and 1950s. Thus, the 2.6 percent productivity trend of the period 1947-67 cannot be taken as representative. Since then, productivity has advanced at just 1.2 percent and has been fading. There was no advance whatsoever in 1977-79 despite the absence of recession.

The international position of U.S. industry has shown a steady deterioration since the late 1950s. The U.S. share in world manufacturing exports has declined sharply as Figure 1 shows. Low-wage, low-productivity industries have been losing ground for half a century, and this is only the logical working of the law of comparative advantage. But the postwar decline of the steel industry, de-

Fig. 1. The U.S. share in world (industrialized countries) manufacturing exports, 1961 to 1977.

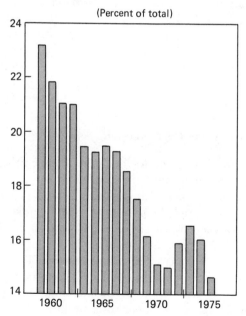

(Percent of total)

Source: Organization for Economic Coordination and Development

spite a relatively good resource base in coal and iron ore and the large domestic market, and the more recent decline of the automobile industry because of cost and product problems raise disturbing questions about our industrial future.

Where has the United States made wrong turns? Can the processes of relative decline be reversed? Or are the historical forces beyond our control so that we had best prepare ourselves for a future of stagnant living standards?

The 1980s are a decisive decade for America's future. The forces of decline can be stemmed through improved understanding, still rapidly advancing technology, capital formation, and improving human resources. But if we fail to come to grips with our problems early in this decade, the United States will wind up taking a back seat to the more disciplined countries such as West Germany, Japan, and possibly to the totalitarian countries developing along socialist lines.

This chapter applies a theoretical and quantitative perspective to our problems and explores some possibilities of economic policies. The study draws on new technology: on econometric models that bring into focus the information and the hypotheses which may explain the information. A tough, quantitative examination rules out magic solutions. But it leaves the door open for orderly, slow-working changes that would reverse the deterioration in the American development process and raise the hope of renewed leadership.

Productivity and Core Inflation

An analysis I prepared for the Joint Economic Committee of the U.S. Congress shows how the current inflation rate developed over the last fifteen years from periods of excess demand, external and internal shocks, and the persistence of core inflation. The central concept of the analysis is core inflation: it is the rate that would occur if the economy were on its long-term equilibrium growth path, free of shocks and excess demand. The core inflation rate reflects those price increases made necessary by increases in the trend costs of the inputs to production, capital, and labor. Since long-term capital and labor costs are heavily affected by price expectations, through wages and interest rates, the core inflation rate is itself largely dependent on the state of expectations. It is also modified by the productivity trend which serves as an offset to rising factor prices of labor. It can be affected by policies which change unit labor and capital costs. Figure 2 shows the core inflation rate and contrasts it to the actual inflation rate. Actual inflation is the sum of core, demand, and shock elements.

The dramatic deterioration of the core inflation rate is, along with energy, the central problem of the economy. Figure 3 shows the origins of the core rate. The problem of core inflation did not originate on the cost side but was created by the prolonged period of excess demand during the Vietnam War when unemployment rates were as low as 3.4 percent and industrial utilization rates were near 90 percent. Excess demand gradually led to an acceleration of wages and, after some further delay, of interest rates and equity costs. As a result, wages and prices were in considerable

Fig. 2.   The core inflation rate and the Consumer Price Index

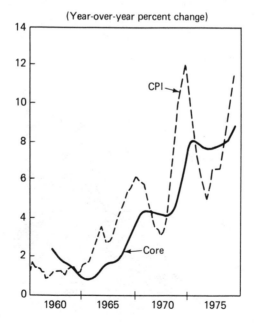

(Year-over-year percent change)

Fig. 3. The origins of core inflation

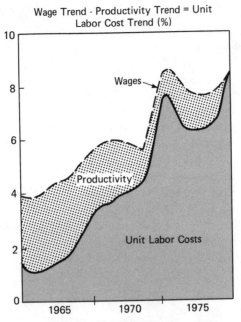

Wage Trend - Productivity Trend = Unit Labor Cost Trend (%)

Wages

Productivity

Unit Labor Costs

1965   1970   1975

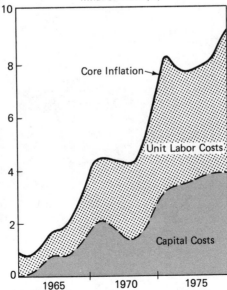

Unit Labor Cost Trend (weight = .65) + Capital Cost Trend (weight = .35) = Core Inflation Rate (%)

Core Inflation

Unit Labor Costs

Capital Costs

1965   1970   1975

motion by 1970 and the core rate had reached 4.4 percent. The recessions of 1970 and 1974-75 brought some temporary relief even to core inflation because of their retarding effect on prices and wages in weak markets. The relief was short-lived as the economy, on each occasion, was returned to a state of excess demand. Further, after 1972, the period of shock inflation began with the initial food price explosion to be followed by the series of OPEC shocks. Payroll tax hikes, the decline of the dollar abroad, and other factors also contributed to a sizable continuing shock inflation rate.

The retardation of productivity also served to substantially worsen core inflation. As Figure 3 shows, productivity became increasingly less able to offset rising wages so that unit labor costs accelerated even more than the rate of wage increase. The drop in productivity growth, and its ultimate cessation, produced a complete conversion of wages into unit labor costs and thereby helped bring the core inflation rate to its 1979 near-9 percent level.

Why Did Productivity Slow Down?

The productivity slowdown has received an enormous amount of analytical attention. Table 1 summarizes two studies using quite different approaches (as well as different measures of productivity). The first is the recently published highly detailed study by Edward F. Denison, accounting for the observed slowdown in national income per person employed. Denison applies his previously developed methodology of decomposing economic growth into its sources. He finds that just over one-third of the productivity slowdown can be attributed to such factors as an accelerated reduction in average hours, a faster shift in the age-sex composition of the labor force, a slower increase in capital per worker, changes in the legal and human environment, the disappearance of gains from reallocation of resources out of farming and nonfarm self-employment, and a slowdown in gains from economies of scale. The remaining two-thirds of the slowdown he leaves in an unexplained, residual series for advances in knowledge and miscellaneous determinants.

Another study, using the econometric method of time series analysis to let each factor indicate its role in the slowdown of nonfarm output per manhour, was conducted by Robin Siegel at Data Resources, Inc. It does not need a residual, but explains the entire

TABLE 1. TWO ANALYSES OF THE PRODUCTIVITY SLOWDOWN (AVERAGE ANNUAL RATES OF CHANGE). THE FIRST ANALYSIS IS DENISON: SOURCES OF GROWTH OF NATIONAL INCOME PER PERSON EMPLOYED, NONRESIDENTIAL BUSINESS SECTOR.

Item	1948–73	1973–76
Growth rate	2.4	—0.5
Irregular factors	—0.2	0.1
Adjusted growth rate	2.6	—0.6
Changes in labor characteristics		
Hours at work	—0.2	—0.5
Age-sex composition	—0.2	—0.3
Education	0.5	0.9
Changes in capital and land per person employed		
Nonresidential structures and equipment	0.3	0.2
Inventories	0.1	0.0
Land	0.0	0.0
Improved allocation of resources	0.4	0.0
Legal and human environment	0.0	—0.4
Economies of scale from larger markets	0.4	0.2
Advances in knowledge and n.e.c.*	1.4	—0.7

* Not elsewhere classified.

Source: Accounting for Slower Economic Growth, *Edward F. Denison, The Brookings Institution, Washington, D.C., 1979.*

THE SECOND ANALYSIS IS SIEGEL: THE COMPOSITION OF GROWTH IN OUTPUT PER MANHOUR, NONFARM BUSINESS SECTOR.

	1973–78	1965–73	1955–65
Time Trend	2.4	2.4	2.4
Economic Utilization	—0.4	0.1	0
Labor Market Tightness	0.2	—0.1	0
Output Surprise	—0.2	0.2	0.2
Energy Prices	—0.7	0	0
Pollution Abatement Expenditures	0	—0.5	0
Output Mix	0	0.1	0
Demographic Composition of Work Force	—0.4	—0.6	—0.6
Capital-Labor Ratio	0	0.7	0.6
Tax Effect	—0.1	—0.3	—0.1
Nonfarm Productivity Growth	0.8	2.0	2.6

Source: "Why Has Productivity Slowed Down?" Robin Siegel, Data Resources Review, *March 1979.*

slowdown by measured factors. The study confirms that the stagnation in the capital-labor ratio after 1973 was perhaps the single largest element in the productivity slowdown. In the preceding twenty-five years, following a pattern set over a whole century, the capital-labor ratio was improving at 2.5 percent a year, indicating the increased amount of capital provided for each worker. The end of this capital deepening has meant that the methods of production have been changing more slowly. If the capital-labor ratio could be made to improve once more, a partial restoration of our traditional productivity performance would be assured.

The demographic factor is also confirmed by the Siegel analysis. The American labor force included increasing numbers of young workers and of women, particularly after 1966. While ultimately likely to have the same productivity as adult men, these groups pose a transitional problem. During their initial years of job experience, they hold positions of lesser skill and lower pay. But the demographic factor should cease to subtract from productivity performance in the years ahead. As Figure 4 shows, the percentage of workers in the below-twenty-four age bracket passed its peak in 1978 and will be dropping even more in the years ahead. The passage of time will make the labor force more seasoned.

The great increase in the number of women workers has more complicated ramifications. The rapidly rising employment ratios for women affect both sides of the labor market. The working woman has a greater demand for services, including meals away from home, personal services, and retailing. She also provides a rapidly growing and elastic supply of labor for these same service occupations. Thus, the sociological factors which are bringing women into the labor force are affecting productivity in ways that require careful interpretation: there is nothing to be decried about a desired rapid growth of service and trade jobs which happens to reduce measured aggregate productivity.

The changing industrial composition of jobs is also a significant element in the productivity slowdown. Denison finds that within the nonfarm, nonresidential business sector this factor has little substance. In terms of job mix he found only the shift of employment from farming to other commodity and service industries to have affected aggregate productivity. However, his conclusions are largely based on research done in 1973. Thurow takes a particu-

Fig. 4.   The share of workers age 16 to 24 in the total labor force

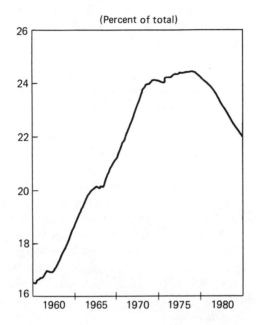

(Percent of total)

larly close look at the recent changes in the effect of industrial mix on productivity. Table 2 shows his estimates of productivity growth by industry. He finds that since 1972, sectoral shifts have been a serious retardant. The most important employment shift is toward services, traditionally a below-average sector for productivity and wages. Enormous growth in the health industry, including nursing homes for the expanding aged population, is one important example. A second important shift is the changing role of agriculture. Earlier in the postwar years, productivity advanced very rapidly in agriculture, and employment shrank in this low productivity sector to help boost the national average. But productivity in agriculture is now above the national average, so that the continuing exit from farms serves to cut aggregate productivity.

The industries with productivity declines are experiencing special circumstances. In the construction industries, the drop is the most dramatic, from +3.4 percent (1948-65) to −0.8 percent (1972-

TABLE 2.   RATES OF PRODUCTIVITY GROWTH BY INDUSTRY (AVERAGE ANNUAL RATES OF CHANGE)

	1948–1965	*1965–1972*	*1972–1977*
Agriculture, Forestry, Fisheries	5.0	4.1	2.4
Mining	4.3	2.4	−5.1
Construction	3.4	−1.8	−0.8
Nondurable Goods Manufacturing	3.3	3.2	2.6
Durable Goods Manufacturing	2.8	2.3	1.3
Transportation	3.1	2.4	2.1
Communications	5.4	4.5	6.5
Electricity, Gas, and Sanitary Services	6.3	3.4	1.0
Wholesale Trade	3.2	4.0	−0.1
Retail Trade	2.6	1.8	1.0
Finance, Insurance, and Real Estate	2.0	0.8	1.4
Services	1.2	1.6	0.2

Source: "The U.S. Productivity Problem," Lester Thurow, Data Resources Review, August 1979.

These 12 industries include 86% of the GNP. The only sector excluded is government, where it is difficult or impossible to measure output. The analysis ends in 1977 since this is the last year for which disaggregate industrial data are available.

77). Thurow questions whether this result is due to difficulties of measurement. Admittedly, the imposition of equal opportunity rules could have some temporary effects on productivity. But the technology in construction is advancing quite rapidly, and the long-established work rules have been diminishing as the percentage of construction performed under union conditions has shrunk. Perhaps it is the low volume of construction, which has barely risen over the last ten years, which is holding back effective resource use.

Two other industries show dramatic declines which can perhaps be explained more readily. The switch in mining from strong positive to strong negative productivity performance is mainly due to the imposition of safety regulations on the coal mining industry. The failure to discover major new sources of oil and gas in the face of a rising volume of drilling also has some small effect on the figures. Finally, the loss of productivity in the electricity, gas, and sanitary services industries from 6.3 percent (1948-65) to 1.0 percent (1972-77) is due to the diminished growth of electricity use because of higher prices.

It is evident that the mix changes, per se, are no particular reason for alarm. A postindustrial society has rapidly rising demands for services and will not show significant increases in employment of manufacturing industries because of the considerable productivity gains of that sector.

Baseline Prospects for the Economy

What are the prospects for the U.S. economy if policies are little changed? A Data Resources, Inc. (DRI) model solution has been developed which makes the following assumptions:

1. OPEC prices increase by 4 percent a year in real terms, i.e., oil rises by the U.S. inflation rate plus 4 percent;
2. The statutory increases in Social Security taxes are allowed to incur, i.e., there is no rollback of the jumps in base and rate of 1981;
3. The federal budget grows by an average of 2.1 percent a year in real terms from 1979 to 1985, with transfer payments to persons growing somewhat more rapidly but grants-in-aid to states showing little increase. The defense budget in these assumptions rises by 2.6 percent a year;
4. Tax policy includes a 1981 reduction of personal and corporate taxes, including some depreciation reform. Thereafter, across-the-board personal income tax cuts slow the increase in the real rate of income taxation from the 1.2 percent of the last decade to 0.6 percent for the first half of the 1980s; and
5. Monetary policy grows nonborrowed bank reserves at 5.9 percent a year, which is sufficient to avoid credit disturbances while holding the growth of monetary aggregates to mildly disinflationary rates.

The simulation also assumes that the 1980 recession is extremely mild, with unemployment rising only to 7.2 percent and dropping to 6 percent in the succeeding two and one-half years of recovery. Personal saving remains at historically low figures, averaging just 4.5 percent.

What would be the prospects for productivity, capital formation, core and actual inflation, financial markets, international trade position, and real activity under these baseline assumptions? Table 3 summarizes the results of a DRI model solution. Highlights for the years 1980-85 include:

1. Potential GNP advances by 2.7 percent, a sharp contrast to the 3.5 percent average of the preceding twenty years;
2. The capital stock increases at a 3.1 percent rate, up from the 2.5 percent rate of the last five years but still well below the 4 percent long-term average;
3. Productivity growth remains sluggish, averaging a 1.4 percent rate of advance;
4. The core inflation rate shows no improvement, indeed worsens to near 9 percent for most of the next five years; the actual inflation rate (CPI) escapes from the current double-digit territory but still remains in the high 8.5–9 percent range;
5. The investment ratio, the percent of nominal GNP plowed back into nonresidential fixed investment, averages 10.8 percent;
6. Real disposable income advances at a 2.9 percent rate, while real income per capita advances 1.9 percent;
7. Housing starts average 1.93 million units, which produces an increase in the nation's housing stock of just 1.6 percent a year;
8. The government deficit averages $19.4 billion a year, or 0.6 percent of GNP (National Income Accounts [NIA] basis);
9. Long-term interest rates, reflecting the high inflation, average 10.34 percent, as measured by AA utility bonds; and
10. Short-term interest rates remain very high as well, with the bank prime rate averaging 11.77 percent.

This baseline simulation may appear pessimistic in terms of some of the long-term trends embodied in it, but it is optimistic in its assumptions about energy and other unpredictable factors. OPEC prices and supplies, agricultural prices, unpredictable elements in consumer and business spending, stop-go policies by the Federal Reserve System or the federal budget, regulatory policies, runs on the dollar, and other such factors could make the path more unstable and thereby also deteriorate the trends significantly. Thus, it is not a worst case, just a trend projection in the absence of major shocks with policies which aim at relatively high resource utilization and do not focus on productivity or capital formation.

TABLE 3. BASELINE PROSPECTS FOR THE U.S. ECONOMY: SUMMARY

	1979	1980	1981	1982	1983	1984	1985
Policy (billions of current $)							
Average Tax Lifetime (years)							
Producers' Durable Equipment	11.1	11.1	9.1	9.1	9.1	9.1	9.1
Nonresidential Structures	22.8	22.8	20.8	20.8	20.8	20.8	20.8
Investment Tax Credit (rate)	0.084	0.086	0.100	0.100	0.100	0.100	0.100
Corporate Profit Tax Accruals	77.5	77.4	87.9	95.1	99.3	108.3	133.0
Macroeconomic Effects (% Ch.)							
Real GNP	2.1	0.0	4.7	3.8	2.3	2.4	3.7
Total Consumption	2.2	0.9	4.3	3.9	2.9	2.5	3.4
Nonres. Fixed Invest.	5.8	−1.9	3.7	6.8	2.1	1.2	4.4
Invest. in Res. Structures	−5.9	−10.3	14.1	6.2	−1.9	1.6	10.8
Net Exports ($bil)	17.4	21.8	23.2	19.7	20.1	24.6	27.3
Government Purchases	0.3	1.5	1.6	2.1	2.2	1.8	1.8
Long-Run Supply (% Ch.)							
Labor Force	2.4	1.6	2.0	2.3	1.7	1.3	1.3
Capital Stock	3.8	3.0	3.1	3.5	3.3	3.0	3.1
Output per Hour	−0.9	0.3	2.2	0.8	0.8	1.7	2.6
Potential GNP	3.1	2.7	2.7	2.7	2.7	2.7	2.7
Inflation and Unemployment (% Ch.)							
Core Inflation Rate	8.7	9.5	8.7	8.6	9.1	9.0	8.5
Consumer Price Index	11.2	10.7	8.2	8.7	8.8	8.5	8.3
Average Hourly Earnings	8.0	8.7	9.2	9.6	9.9	9.9	10.0
Real Wages	−0.8	−0.4	0.8	1.0	1.2	1.5	1.9
Unemployment Rate (rate)	5.9	7.0	6.7	6.1	6.1	6.2	6.0
Capacity Utilization (rate)	0.854	0.815	0.851	0.872	0.854	0.838	0.852
Financial Markets							
Rental Price of Capital (% Ch.)	10.2	8.2	10.4	14.8	11.1	7.3	7.6
Prime Rate (rate)	12.72	12.84	10.61	11.82	12.44	11.99	10.92
New High-Grade Corp. Bond Rate (rate)		9.88	10.43	9.93	10.42	10.59	10.45	10.23

Responsibilities and Limits of Demand Management

What would it take to reduce the core inflation rate through tougher demand management alone, given the apparently inescapable push from shock inflation? Table 4 summarizes a model solution in which the core inflation rate is brought down by one percentage point by 1985. To achieve this gain in the core inflation rate requires an increment of average unemployment of over 2 percent by 1985. Thus, demand management would have to aim at an unemployment rate of 8 percent following the small 1980-81 recession.

It is disappointing that the trade-off between unemployment and core inflation is only two to one even after five years, but it should not be all that surprising in light of the analysis. The economy's problems are not really solved except for the elimination of excessively aggressive fiscal and monetary policies. The imbalance between the supply of labor and capital continues so that the utilization rate of industry averages 82 percent in the years 1982-85 even though unemployment averages 7.9 percent. The unemployment level is clearly deflationary, but the utilization rate of physical capital is not far from its equilibrium rate. In other words, the imbalance in the structure of production, in which there is an inadequate supply of basic industrial capacity compared to the supply of labor, continues to be damaging and limits the benefits of holding down aggregate demand. Lack of improvement is also due to the continuing shocks to the system from energy which indirectly serve to raise the equilibrium rate of unemployment.

Figure 5 shows the results of other simulations to define the 1985 trade-off between demand management and inflation. The reader may be surprised to find a curve that still looks suspiciously like a Phillips curve. But it should be noted that with the traditional aggressive demand management policies which aim to hold unemployment below 6 percent, there really is no trade-off; the inflation rate deteriorates very dramatically so that the Phillips curve ultimately does become vertical. However, at the more moderate demand management ranges that are explored more thoroughly in

TABLE 4. THE EFFECTS OF DEMAND MANAGEMENT ON CORE INFLATION [1]
RESULTING ECONOMY: SUMMARY (PERCENT CHANGE)

	1979	1980	1981	1982	1983	1984	1985
Core Inflation Rate	8.7	9.5	8.6	8.3	8.5	8.1	7.5
Real GNP (1972 Dollars)	2.1	−1.0	2.6	2.7	1.7	1.8	2.8
Total Consumption	2.2	0.1	2.4	2.5	2.0	1.7	2.3
Nonres. Fixed Invest.	5.8	−2.4	1.7	5.7	3.1	2.3	4.7
Invest. in Res. Structures	−5.9	−10.5	15.1	12.1	6.2	7.1	9.9
Net Exports ($bil)	17.4	21.6	25.5	25.9	28.1	34.5	39.8
Government Purchases	0.3	−0.6	−1.8	−1.4	−1.2	−1.3	−0.9
Imported Fuel Price	38.5	33.4	12.0	11.2	10.4	10.2	10.0
Personal Consumption Deflator	8.9	9.1	8.3	8.3	8.0	7.5	6.9
Output per Hour	−0.9	−0.1	1.5	0.6	1.0	1.7	2.3
Potential GNP	3.1	2.7	2.6	2.5	2.5	2.5	2.6
Unemployment Rate (rate)	5.9	7.2	7.6	7.5	7.7	8.0	8.1
Capacity Utilization (level)	0.854	0.804	0.814	0.831	0.822	0.808	0.811

THE CHANGE FROM THE BASELINE CASE

	1979	1980	1981	1982	1983	1984	1985
Difference in rate of change							
Core Inflation Rate	0.0	0.0	−0.1	−0.3	−0.6	−0.9	−1.0
Percent Difference							
Real GNP (1972 Dollars)	0.0	−1.0	−3.0	−4.0	−4.6	−5.1	−6.0
Total Consumption	0.0	−0.7	−2.5	−3.8	−4.7	−5.5	−6.5
Nonres. Fixed Invest.	0.0	−0.5	−2.4	−3.4	−2.4	−1.3	−1.0
Invest. in Res. Structures	0.0	−0.2	0.6	6.2	15.0	21.3	20.3
Net Exports	0.0	−0.8	10.1	31.4	39.9	40.1	46.0
Government Purchases	0.0	−2.1	−5.4	−8.7	−11.8	−14.4	−16.8
Imported Fuel Price	0.0	0.0	0.0	−0.3	−0.9	−1.6	−2.5
Personal Consumption Deflator	0.0	0.0	0.0	−0.3	−0.9	−1.6	−2.5
Output per Hour	0.0	−0.4	−1.2	−1.4	−1.2	−1.2	−1.5
Potential GNP	0.0	0.0	−0.1	−0.2	−0.4	−0.6	−0.7
Unemployment Rate [2]	0.0	0.2	0.9	1.4	1.6	1.8	2.1
Capacity Utilization [2]	0.00	−0.01	−0.04	−0.04	−0.03	−0.03	−0.04

[1] *Results of simulation designed to lower the core inflation rate 1 percent by 1985.*

[2] *Difference in level*

Fig. 5. The effect of demand management on core inflation

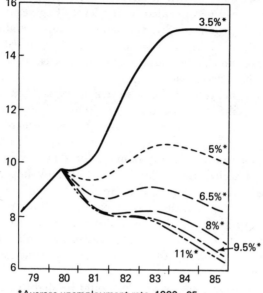

Core Inflation Rate Under Different Economic Conditions

*Average unemployment rate, 1980 - 85

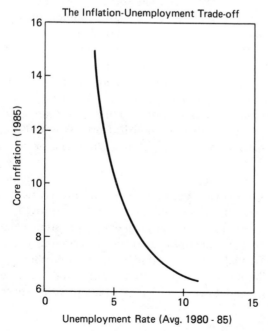

The Inflation-Unemployment Trade-off

this exercise, there is a trade-off even after five years: the increase in the price level is controlled by the level of aggregate demand in relation to aggregate supply, and policy retains the ability to vary aggregate demand in accordance with the permitted increase in bank reserves and money supply and the degree of stimulus originating in the federal budget.

The curve shows that the achievement of a dramatically lower core inflation rate by 1985, in the 6 percent area, requires the maintenance of near depression conditions. Unemployment would have to be well over 10 percent from now until then, an economic condition which would seriously damage the economy in other ways, probably radicalize the electorate, and thereby imperil the capitalist system as we know it. Even to achieve more moderate anti-inflation goals through demand management alone poses only discouraging prospects. If the unemployment rate were maintained near 8 percent from 1980 to 1985, inflation would be improved, but the core rate would still be near 7.5 percent at the end of the experiment.

Actual inflation rates, of course, would be slightly more sensitive to the higher unemployment than the core because of the more immediate offset provided by the demand component of inflation. However, actual inflation also includes shock pressures and, although the weaker domestic economy might tone down OPEC pricing strategy modestly, the energy problem could hardly be expected to disappear. Thus, with 8 percent unemployment, the Consumer Price Index still increases at a 7 percent rate; even 10 percent unemployment does not produce less than a 6 percent CPI. It is very dubious that the political process would accept such political strategy, regardless of who is President or which party controls the Congress.

In summary, the fiscal and monetary policies which the government employs to manage aggregate demand must create a constructive environment in which inflation can be improved, but they cannot, by themselves, solve the problem. Aggressive demand management, aiming at unemployment rates averaging 6 percent or less every year, make it impossible to have any other policy succeed. The inflation will simply become worse and worse—until the public despairs and forces politicians to adopt price controls. But even if demand management sets its gauges to achieve unemployment in the 6.5 to 7 percent area, the inflation problem is not solved. Indeed, given the probable shocks from energy, with a real OPEC increase of 4 percent a year, there would be no improvement in the core inflation rate. These exercises demonstrate that demand management must be careful and somewhat more conservative than it has been, but that it is beyond its capacities to accomplish an adequate improvement of inflation.

What Should We Expect From Supply-Oriented Policies?

The range of policies that can be considered is very large, and it would clearly be beyond the scope of this chapter to explore them all. Let me focus on only two major areas: capital formation through tax incentives, and energy.

Tax Incentives for Capital Formation and Their Effects on Productivity

Here let me report on a composite tax policy simulation which incorporates both a more generous investment tax credit and a more liberal depreciation scheme. The specific assumptions are a 3 percent increase in the effective tax credit and a two-year cut in the average tax lifetime of producers' plant and equipment. The direct loss of corporate tax revenue is $16 billion almost immediately and $30 billion by 1985. Of this revenue loss, 12 percent is recaptured through the feedback effects of a stronger economy. The stimulus to investment is quite considerable, slightly exceeding the revenue loss for a few years. Table 5 summarizes the results. With the capital stock 3.1 percent bigger by 1985, the level of potential GNP is enhanced by 2 percent and productivity is 2.4 percent higher. With the rental price of capital favorably affected by the tax moves, core inflation improves early on, and is improved by 0.8 percent by 1985.

This improvement is obviously not the entire solution to the

TABLE 5 (A). THE EFFECTS OF TAX INCENTIVES ON CORE INFLATION
THE RESULTING ECONOMY: SUMMARY

	1979	1980	1981	1982	1983	1984	1985
Policy (billions of current $)							
Average Tax Lifetime (years)							
Producers' Durable Equipment	11.1	9.1	7.1	7.1	7.1	7.1	7.1
Nonresidential Structures	22.8	20.8	18.8	18.8	18.8	18.8	18.8
Investment Tax Credit (rate)	0.084	0.116	0.130	0.130	0.130	0.130	0.130
Corporate Profit Tax Accruals	77.5	65.6	76.5	80.2	77.2	82.8	106.4
Macroeconomic Effects (% Ch.)							
Real GNP	2.1	0.1	5.2	3.9	2.1	2.8	4.4
Total Consumption	2.2	0.9	4.3	3.8	2.7	2.8	3.9
Nonres. Fixed Invest.	5.8	−1.7	8.0	9.6	1.5	1.4	6.1
Invest. in Res. Structures	−5.9	−9.4	16.6	3.0	−3.2	3.7	15.4
Net Exports ($bil)	17.4	22.0	23.0	19.6	20.2	24.9	27.6
Government Purchases	0.3	1.6	1.6	2.1	2.4	1.8	1.7
Long-Run Supply (% Ch.)							
Labor Force	2.4	1.6	2.0	2.3	1.7	1.3	1.3
Capital Stock	3.8	3.1	3.6	4.3	3.8	3.5	3.8
Output per Hour	−0.9	0.4	2.8	1.1	1.0	2.3	3.2
Potential GNP	3.1	2.8	2.9	3.1	3.3	3.2	3.0
Inflation and Unemployment (% Ch.)							
Core Inflation Rate	8.7	9.3	8.0	8.0	8.4	8.2	7.7
Consumer Price Index	11.2	10.6	8.2	8.7	8.6	8.1	7.9
Average Hourly Earnings	8.0	8.7	9.2	9.6	9.8	9.6	9.6
Real Wages	−0.8	−0.4	0.9	1.1	1.2	1.6	2.0
Unemployment Rate (rate)	5.9	7.0	6.6	6.0	6.3	6.6	6.3
Capacity Utilization (level)	0.854	0.815	0.865	0.884	0.849	0.831	0.853
Financial Markets (% Ch.)							
Rental Price of Capital	10.2	1.5	10.8	15.9	9.3	5.2	7.6
Prime Rate (rate)	12.72	12.32	10.32	12.56	13.00	11.62	10.52
New High-Grade Corp.							
Bond Rate (rate)	9.88	10.51	10.42	11.35	11.47	11.01	10.63

TABLE 5 (B). THE CHANGE FROM THE BASELINE CASE

	1979	1980	1981	1982	1983	1984	1985
Policy							
Difference in Level							
Average Tax Lifetime (years)							
Producers' Durable Equipment	0.0	−2.0	−2.0	−2.0	−2.0	−2.0	−2.0
Nonresidential Structures	0.0	−2.0	−2.0	−2.0	−2.0	−2.0	−2.0
Investment Tax Credit (rate)	0.000	0.030	0.030	0.030	0.030	0.030	0.030
Macroeconomic Effects							
Percent Difference							
Real GNP	0.0	0.1	0.6	0.7	0.5	0.8	1.5
Total Consumption	0.0	0.0	0.0	−0.2	−0.3	0.0	0.5
Nonres. Fixed Invest.	0.0	0.2	4.3	7.1	6.5	6.7	8.5
Invest. in Res. Structures	0.0	1.1	3.3	0.2	−1.1	0.9	5.1
Net Exports	0.0	1.0	−0.7	−0.9	0.6	1.1	1.1
Government Purchases	0.0	0.1	0.1	0.0	0.2	0.2	0.1
Long-Run Supply							
Percent Difference							
Labor Force	0.0	0.0	0.0	0.0	0.0	−0.1	−0.1
Capital Stock	0.0	0.0	0.6	1.3	1.9	2.4	3.1
Output per Hour	0.0	0.1	0.6	1.0	1.2	1.8	2.4
Potential GNP	0.0	0.0	0.2	0.6	1.2	1.7	2.0
Inflation and Unemployment							
Percent Difference							
Core Inflation Rate *	0.0	−0.2	−0.6	−0.7	−0.7	−0.8	−0.8
Consumer Price Index	0.0	−0.1	−0.1	−0.1	−0.3	−0.7	−1.1
Average Hourly Earnings	0.0	0.0	0.0	0.0	−0.1	−0.4	−0.7
Real Wages	0.0	0.1	0.2	0.3	0.3	0.4	0.5
Unemployment Rate (diff. in level)	0.0	0.0	−0.1	−0.1	0.2	0.3	0.2
Capacity Utilization (diff. in level)	0.000	0.000	0.014	0.012	−0.006	−0.007	0.001
Financial Markets							
Difference in Level							
Rental Price of Capital (% diff.)	0.0	−6.1	−5.8	−4.9	−6.4	−8.2	−8.2
Prime Rate	0.00	−0.52	−0.29	0.74	0.56	−0.37	−0.41
New High-Grade Corp. Bond Rate	0.00	0.08	0.49	0.93	0.88	0.56	0.40

* *Difference in rate of change*

Fig. 6. The effect of tax incentives on core inflation

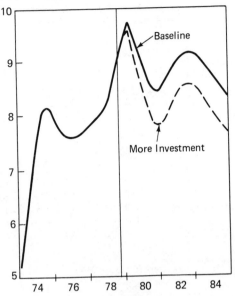

* *Assumes a 3 percent increase in the investment tax credit and a two-year cut in the average tax lifetime of producers' plant and equipment relative to base.*

inflation problem, but at least it begins to make a dent and creates a more realistic possibility that the tide can be turned.

The Energy Issue and Inflation

The preceding discussion has assumed that OPEC prices will rise by a full 4 percent a year in addition to the rise in the aggregate price level. There is now a lively controversy whether the 1979 imbalance in world oil markets is the beginning of a new era of genuine oil shortage, with OPEC countries curtailing production in order to husband scarce resources, or whether the shortage was manipulated by the short-run revenue maximizing constraints of a cleverly conspiring cartel. Whatever the truth may be, there is no reason to believe that the power of OPEC will weaken. Consequently, if the real price of energy is to be held to the 4 percent path, U.S. imports must be brought down.

Figure 7 shows the projected oil import bill for this country. It can be seen that the outlay of $43 billion of 1978 reaches $81 billion in 1980, $112 billion in 1982, and $167 billion by 1985. Figure 8 shows the oil import bill in relation to nominal GNP, portraying clearly that it is a rising burden. It is hard to envisage an adaptation by U.S. industry that would boost our exports by comparable sums. Consequently, the oil bill projection implies growing international deficits on current account which would have to be offset by capital movements. The dollar overhang that would be created by this projection would inevitably keep pressure on the foreign exchange rate of the dollar and contribute to the continuation of the inflation process itself. High U.S. demands for oil will also contribute to a relatively tight world oil situation, encouraging

Fig. 7. The fuel import bill

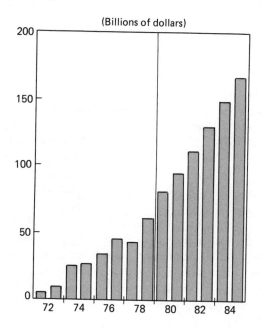

(Billions of dollars)

Fig. 8. The fuel import bill as a percent of GNP

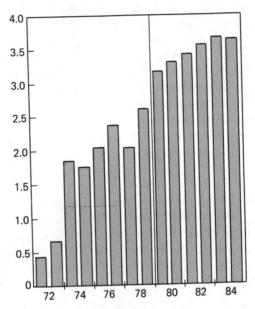

OPEC (or individual members) to disrupt supplies at little economic risk.

It is important to see the role of energy in the inflationary process in a historical perspective. Energy has been a major, but not exclusive, cause of the present inflation. Figure 9 shows the results of a model simulation in which the actual inflation performance is compared with a hypothetical test in which the price of energy would have risen no more rapidly than other prices. It can be seen that the inflation rate would be about a quarter less over the time span.

Figure 10 repeats the same exercise looking into the future. If real energy prices could be kept stable, the prospects for improvement in the core inflation rate would be substantially better. A combination of antiinflationary policies—conservative demand management plus tax incentives to investment plus conservation and supply policies that would hold the real price of OPEC constant—would produce a more dramatic improvement in the core inflation rate, as well as in the actual inflation rate, of course.

Fig. 9. *The effect of energy prices on inflation: a historical perspective (Core inflation rate, history compared to results of hypothetical test in which energy prices rise no more rapidly than other prices)*

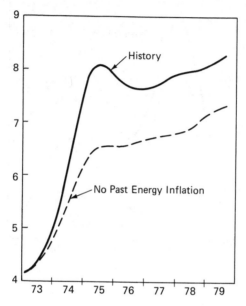

Fig. 10.   The effect of energy prices on inflation: future prospects (Core inflation rate, baseline prospects compared to results of simulation assuming no real energy price inflation)

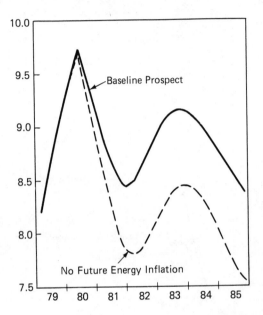

Robert C. Holland

4

Public and Private Sector Working Relations

Introduction

The President of the United States leads a nation with unparalleled material and intellectual resources and a remarkable record of achievement. Yet we have entered the decade of the 1980s with a combined sense of disappointment, frustration, and inability to cope with our problems that is unusual in our history.

Why is this so? Partly it may reflect the unrealistic height to which our aspirations and expectations soared in the decades following World War II. Partly the trouble stems from the changing characteristics of our problems. Not many of them are brand new, but some have grown a great deal in size, and we now perceive their present harm and portents much more clearly. Furthermore, in this increasingly interdependent society, our major problems are proving to be more complex, more interrelated, and more intractable than we earlier thought.

ROBERT C. HOLLAND *is president of the Committee for Economic Development (CED), a research and educational organization devoted to the study of public policy problems. Prior to joining the CED, Dr. Holland held a variety of positions at the Federal Reserve System, culminating in service as a member of its Board of Governors.*

But surely one of the major causes of our shortcomings is the inadequacy of our institutions. The organizations and processes installed in our society to manage our resources and deal with our problems have all too often not measured up to their tasks. Design failures, misconceived goals, and faulty execution have plagued them. Furthermore, because they have been typically slow to change —even hidebound—and oriented to already demonstrated problems, many of our major institutions have been rendered obsolescent in one degree or another by the accelerating pace of change today. Aggravating these other weaknesses has been a tendency for misunderstanding and antagonism to develop between institutions, inhibiting their ability to mount cooperative attacks on problems. Nowhere has this tendency been more apparent than between two of the institutions in which society has lodged much of its power— government and business. This troubled interface between business and government is the focus of the body of this chapter.

A WORD ON SCOPE AND DEFINITIONS

A certain degree of simplification of presentation seems advisable in order to keep this chapter of manageable length and sharpen the points of discussion. Thus, the term "government" will ordinarily be used as if it describes a monolithic institution. In fact, of course, the public sector contains a large assortment of government entities—federal, state, and local; executive, legislative, and judicial. The connections between them range from the rigidly hierarchical to the virtually nonexistent. References to specific parts of government are inserted by the author wherever they seem particularly relevant to the analysis. The reader is invited to supply as many additional associations out of his or her own experience as seem useful.

Similarly, the private sector contains a vast array of organizations, many of which are very important in the application of resources to society's problems. Among them are trade unions, nonprofit organizations, civic organizations, community groups, church-based institutions, and privately funded educational institutions. Even within the private institution called business, there is a congeries of organizations of contrasting sizes, skills, and product or service specializations. Here also references to specific kinds of private sector organizations will be introduced wherever they seem particularly helpful in illuminating the point; and the reader is invited to add references at will. The basic part of the private sector on which the rest of the chapter focuses, however, will be business, as the chief manager of private sector resources.

Government and Business: An Adversary History

The history of relations between American government and business is a tempestuous one. Each has appeared as a perennial critic of the other. Yet businesses have repeatedly sought government protection or assistance; and government regularly depends upon business for most of its purchased materials and services— and for a good bit of its tax revenues.

What then are the underlying causes of the adversary tone that pervades so much of United States business-government interchange? Is it rooted in inherent conflicts between two such centers of power? Is it the legacy of the fierce yearning for free and unfettered activity that has sparked our country from its beginning? Or is it the product of latter-day trespasses by each on territory that the other feels responsible for defending? Is it caused or aggravated by personal differences, or by the litigious nature of much of our machinery for resolving differences?

The answers to questions such as these would help clarify whether this business-government antagonism is a permanent characteristic that must be endured, or an attitude that can be corrected. Some evidence can be found in support of affirmative answers to each of the foregoing questions. A brief review of American history may facilitate judgments as to which influences should be accorded the greater weight.

As distinguished a historian as Harvard's Alfred Chandler dates the manifestation of a generally adversarial relationship between business and government in this country in the latter part of the nineteenth century.

The earliest wide-scale efforts by government to regulate business took place after the Civil War. Economic growth and the development of the frontier in the western part of the nation were spurred in the main by private individuals and companies. The competition between companies was fierce, sometimes unprincipled, and occasionally ended with the takeover of one by another. In this manner, the key growth areas of the economy toward the end of the 1800s—transportation, communications, electric and gas utilities, and other major industrials—tended to become dominated by large private companies, the fittest who had survived.

Into this maelstrom of competition and industrial development of the late nineteenth century stepped the public sector, particularly the federal and state governments. In many cases perceived abuses were serious, and a dampening of the extreme "anything goes" climate was called for. But the earliest targets of public regulation were the large and powerful business hierarchies whose size, difficult as it is to fathom in our day, dwarfed even that of the federal government. (As Chandler and others have pointed out, in 1890, when the total federal civilian and military labor force numbered just 60,000 persons, at least a dozen railroads employed over 100,000 workers each.)

The earliest major efforts of government were to regulate and control some of these large business entities. The Interstate Commerce Commission, created in 1887, is commonly considered the bellwether for modern U.S. forms of government regulation of the private sector. The ICC's establishment was closely followed, in 1890, by the Sherman Antitrust Act which struck at a powerful avenue of corporate expansion. Soon after came the first attempts, by both the federal and state governments, to regulate the emerging suppliers of electricity and communication. Food and drug laws and related types of regulation came into being around the turn of the century as well.

It is interesting to note what these diverse forms of regulation had in common. First, the regulatory technique used from the outset was the "command and control" variety, about which we hear so many complaints today. Such measures were commonly directed at limiting prices, market share, profit margin, unfair or unsound practices, and takeover attempts deemed inhibitive of competition. Second, the regulatory appeal process generally involved quasi-judicial procedures in commission hearings (and eventually in courts themselves). The appeals, in other words, relied on U.S.-style types of conflict resolution which attempt to establish the facts of a case through an adversarial process. Participants in such proceedings were thus encouraged to exaggerate their differences in the extreme arguments, leaving it to adjudicative authorities to find any reasonable ground between the two.

Regulatory enforcement was complicated by America's unique republican form of government with its division of powers between states and the national government. In the early heyday of regulation, there was little if any coordination between federal and state agencies engaged in regulating the same industry; often, the same company was beseiged by conflicting commands and controls simultaneously. Consequently, jurisdictional disputes between federal and state agencies did much to complicate an already antagonistic climate of interaction between business and government. And it was made even more complex by rapid turnover in the agencies, by ease of political influence, and by conflicts within the business community, some segments of which (e.g., small businessmen) often favored and promoted regulatory and antitrust measures against "big business."

NEW ROLES FOR GOVERNMENT: THE POST-WORLD WAR II ERA

Predominantly since 1945, new forms and magnitudes of government intervention in the economy have developed, impelled by broader environmental and social concerns among the citizenry. These new interventions have led to increased conflicts with the private sector. Antagonisms have been heightened by government programs and policies that affect not only the general economic climate but also extend into previously internal affairs of private firms.

Permeating the new regulatory climate is a new emphasis on the achievement of social goals through regulation and other actions by government. Environmental laws now influence practically the entire spectrum of industrial activity. Occupational health and safety requirements, in tandem with equal employment and affirmative action laws, have had massive impacts on U.S. business.

Social target setting increasingly suffuses government spending and hiring, the magnitude and impact of which have grown dramatically since 1945. Employees of government in 1979 comprised over 17 percent of the civilian work force. Government expenditures have grown to one-third of the nation's GNP. Public sector borrowing, extensions of credit, and loan guarantees have thrust government into a new role in the financial markets. Rapid expansion of subsidies and differential tax arrangements have had untold consequences on market and production decisions. And finally, the gradual growth of government owned and operated enterprises (e.g., railroads, urban mass transit, rental housing, transport terminal facilities, military commissaries, toll highways, irrigation, and drinking water supply, to name a few) has led to what some would consider "unfair" competition with private companies engaged in similar activities.

Deepening government involvement in the economy and in day-to-day affairs of the private sector is a fundamental change whose long-term consequences will be substantial. The public sector not only sets the rules of the economic game but increasingly has become a player itself. The development of public-private competition in the short term has already contributed much to public sector-private sector frictions.

THE GROWING GAP BETWEEN POLITICS AND ECONOMICS

Finally, the antagonism between business and the public sector —which many knowledgeable observers argue seriously worsened in the 1960s and 1970s—reflects a growing gulf between domestic political forces to which a democratic government must respond and the long-term economic forces impacting business.

Carl Kaysen and others have persuasively outlined post-World War II trends in the political process. American society is experiencing what Kaysen calls a broad "democratization," a basic change in the character of the political process. Political parties are declining (there are now more Independents than registered Republicans), to be supplanted by single-issue groups and political entrepreneurs. The rising level of education among the electorate has led to greater activism and orientation toward particular issues, usually of immediate concern. There has been gradually increased legitimacy accorded to the "entitlement" view of economic benefits, creating pressure for equality of condition rather than equality of opportunity and increased expectations that government should legislate such equality. Lastly, the predominance of the electronic media in supplying information to voters and constituents has caused a new focus on appearance and the "newsworthy negative" in politics, frequently to the detriment of substance and issues of long-term consequence to the nation's economy.

Alongside these emergent changes in the political process, the market economy in the last two decades has been buffeted and altered by a variety of forces that have led some to call for more, not less, centralized direction. High inflation combined with consistently high unemployment and sluggish economic growth is, of course, the central problem affecting the economic decisions of government, business, and the individual alike. The incredible multiplication of the price of energy since 1974 has caused a major redirection of resources within the market economy. In the domestic labor force, we are witnessing the beginnings of some basic shifts —in the demography of the worker pool, the slowly increasing ratio of nonwork to work, and the changing character of jobs. Each of these developments requires adjustments in the economy and in business.

On the international front, the U.S. is still somewhat disoriented from uncertainties stemming from elimination of the gold standard, the advent of floating exchange rates, and the decline of the U.S. dollar. During the 1980s, the less developed nations of Africa, Asia, Latin America, and the Middle East will become increasingly important to the U.S. economy, and trade policy adjustments will have to be made. Finally, the U.S. will have to adapt to increasing international interdependence, which widens the exposure of nations to economic forces originating elsewhere, at a time when nation-states are trying to act more and more as purposeful economic units.

In general, the U.S. political process operates with a shorter time horizon (e.g., two, four, and at most, six-year election cycles) than the time frame necessary to address our most serious economic problems. It tends to resist policy decisions whose benefits are long-term but whose political costs must be paid by the next election. To improve working relations between government and business, some closing of this gap must be achieved. It is the source of much misunderstanding and antagonism, and threatens to disrupt the consensus-building this nation will require to achieve economic and social improvement in the 1980s.

Constructive Public-Private Sector Working Relationships

Having cited influences that might continue to foster poor relations between the public and private sectors, let us turn to consideration of procedures that might produce a more congenial result.

Should we place our chief hope on new elements of understanding emerging through conventional governing procedures? One can imagine the winners of future elections being individuals with more understanding of economic problems and how they could best be dealt with. One can also imagine future chief executive officers of companies more often being individuals with increased comprehension of government objectives and processes. Better election campaigns and a more broadly educated citizenry could help with the former. Well-informed business spokesmen could have plenty of opportunities to both contribute and gain better mutual understanding by engaging in congressional testimony and public discussions that contain more accurate, relevant, and balanced information and are more clearly oriented to be consistent with the public interest. Even business pleadings before the courts and regulatory agencies could partake more of this character. With perhaps an equal or even greater stretch of the imagination, one could conceive of government officials more often foregoing rhetorical excess and, instead, stating the two (or more) sides of pending issues in harmonizing rather than polarizing terms. One could even imagine more candid efforts on the part of officials to describe problems and invite well-intentioned counsel on how best to deal with them.

It may well be, however, that the path to more cooperative business-government working relationships will be blazed chiefly by innovative procedures apart from the traditional hierarchies of public and private sector decision making. Arrangements can be seen springing up here and there throughout the country, typically in the form of ad hoc coalitions to attack particular local or regional problems more effectively. They vary in form and style, demonstrating a kind of native ingenuity in designing around obstacles with an eye firmly fixed on the intended objective. By reviewing some key examples of them, however, one may be able to discern certain common elements that could be carried forward to more generalized applications.

TRAINING AND HIRING THE HARD-TO-EMPLOY

The persistence of undesirably high rates of both unemployment and inflation in the late 1970s prompted renewed interest in non-inflationary ways of finding jobs for the hard-to-employ. A search across the country by the Committee for Economic Development (CED) and other organizations turned up numerous businesses that were engaged in novel programs to train the hard-to-employ to help meet their own labor force needs. These programs were often encouraged, and sometimes partly supported, by government man-power agencies. At the urging of public and private sector groups, the federal government was persuaded to allocate a portion of its massive CETA outlays ($11 billion in fiscal 1978) to induce greater private sector involvement and new public-private partnership programs for the hard-to-employ, while still giving support to ex-isting efforts to combat this problem.

Common Elements—The range of business programs to recruit, train, place, retain, and promote the hard-to-employ is very wide. It runs the gamut from heavy industry to the service sector; from small, family-owned enterprises to some of the nation's largest cor-porations; and from programs to prepare young people for the world of work to those aimed at retaining older workers in pro-ductive jobs. Programs are tailored to talented minority youth, ex-offenders, the handicapped, the mentally disabled, and individ-uals entering the workforce for the first time. And significantly, such programs are found in all regions of the nation.

Within all this variety are a number of common principles. Typi-cally, private sector programs for the hard-to-employ are: (a) car-ried out with little fanfare, (b) based on anticipatory analysis of a firm's labor needs over the long haul, and (c) treated as manage-ment problems to be implemented by a properly trained and motivated human resources staff working with line managers and with close monitoring to assure that cost, retention, and other ob-jectives are met. In sum, these efforts are based on hard-headed *economic* principles—enlightened private sector self-interest as op-posed to a nebulous notion of what is the socially responsible thing to do. In microcosm, they demonstrate the marriage of economic concerns and social goals, or what Charles Schultze, chairman of

President Carter's Council of Economic Advisors, called the harnessing of private interest for the public good.

To help in training and hiring the hard-to-employ, the private sector increasingly is turning to public-private "intermediary" organizations. Such agencies, sponsored by consortia of companies, community groups, or national nonprofit organizations, provide specialized backup to employers. Intermediaries can handle counseling, placement, paperwork needed for public subsidies, and related support tasks, freeing the employer to concentrate on training the hard-to-employ individual. Intermediary agency backup often proves crucial in gaining the support and cooperation of line managers who must provide the actual on-the-job supervision and training.

A model intermediary organization is the Chicago Alliance of Business Manpower Services (CABMS). Using federal job training funds channeled through the Chicago city government, CABMS contracts with area employers for on-the-job commitments, then refers trainees to the firm under contract. The employer benefits from a partial subsidy for training he might not otherwise afford and is furnished needy and motivated trainees who can do the job. The CABMS process is highly cost-effective, and benefits from tight management and strong links to diverse constituencies in the Chicago community, including business, minority groups, and the city administration.

Varied examples can be found across the country:

1. A national intermediary organization with affiliates in forty-seven states is Opportunities Industrialization Centers of America, Inc. (OIC). The largest training employment and training agency in the nation except for the U.S. Department of Labor, OIC has had notable success in serving employers and the minority jobless alike. By providing skill training, counseling, and placement to enrollees for job openings in fields or individual firms which are known to need workers, OIC helped place many formerly hard-to-employ individuals in productive, unsubsidized jobs. The effectiveness of OIC stems from a strong public-private partnership approach, bolstered by government financial support, business private sector training expertise, and strong backing from local communities.

2. A Union Carbide plant in Oak Ridge, Tennessee, participates in a program for training skilled workers called Training and Technology (TAT). With administrative backup supplied by the Oak Ridge Asso-

ciated Universities, Union Carbide prepares the hard-to-employ, including migrant workers, for available jobs. The company treats trainees no differently from regular employees, and trainee work is strictly judged by plant foremen. The important ingredient in the success of the TAT program appears to be individualized instruction by experienced craftsmen in a regular industrial setting.

3. On the West Coast, two intermediary agencies work to serve the job needs of older workers. In the San Francisco Bay area, Retirement Jobs, Inc. helped over 12,000 older workers and retirees find jobs in 1978. The Second Careers Program, founded in Los Angeles in 1975, helps Southern California firms improve their retirement counseling while assisting older workers in finding postretirement careers or establishing their own small businesses.

4. Also working with the young is a coalition of firms which supports the High School Academies program in Philadelphia schools. The academies are "schools within schools" which train potential dropouts in the electrical, automotive, and business fields.

5. Some firms have set up programs for the hard-to-employ with minimal or no outside help. The General Electric Company has a variety of forward-looking policies to relieve future skill shortages. One of GE's efforts entails "educating the educators" by bringing secondary school teachers and guidance counselors into company plants for brief periods during summer vacation periods. Texas Instruments cultivates future engineering talent by participating in a work-study program in several Dallas, Texas, schools. The Koppers Company, engaged in school-to-work programs, discovered that employees who had the chance to work with young people gained from the experience as well.

Public Sector Support for Private Sector Initiatives—To its credit, the public sector, especially the federal government, did much in the late 1970s to facilitate private involvement in helping the hard-to-employ. On-the-job training subsidies were a major contribution. In addition, tax measures passed during this period favorably altered the costs of taking on new low-skilled workers. The Targeted Jobs Tax Credit, one such incentive, allows employers to claim credits up to a maximum of $4,500 over two years for wages paid to seven categories of the disadvantaged. The Federal Revenue Act of 1978 liberalized write-off provisions for companies that hire welfare recipients. In 1978, Congress also created incentives for companies to upgrade workers, including the disadvantaged, by broadening deductions for employer-paid tuition and related educational expenses.

A major sign of the changing times is the newest section of the

Comprehensive Employment and Training Act, Title VII, otherwise known as the Private Sector Initiative Program (PSIP). PSIP constitutes an important attempt by the federal government to begin shifting the emphasis in publicly funded job programs from public service employment (usually providing little real skill training and no permanent career path) to productive training and eventually unsubsidized positions in the private sector. Title VII requires local CETA agencies to establish advisory groups, comprised primarily of business representatives, in order to receive PSIP funds. Known as Private Industry Councils—PICS—these local groups have a broad mandate to design and carry out training programs for the unemployed; the sole requirement is that private employers provide the training. As of August 1979, 335 of the 460 local CETA agencies in the United States had set up PICs in order to qualify for private sector job training funds.

The Private Sector Initiative Program is a major step forward. It puts business and government together in a new partnership to train the unemployed for productive jobs in business and industry. President Carter chose to announce the program in his 1978 annual *Economic Report of the President,* saying:

> Five out of every six new jobs in the economy are created in the private sector. There are good reasons for continuing to rely mainly on the private sector in the years ahead. By emphasizing the creation of private jobs, our resources will be used more efficiently, our future capacity to produce will expand more rapidly, and the standard of living for our people will rise faster. Reliance upon the private sector does not mean neglecting the tasks that government can and must perform. The federal government can be an active partner to help achieve progress toward meeting national needs and, through competent management, still absorb a declining portion of the nation's output. . . .
>
> Government programs can provide valuable assistance to the unemployed. In the end, however, we must turn to the private sector for the bulk of permanent job opportunities for the disadvantaged. It is in private industry that most productive jobs with opportunity for advancement are found.

Thus was a new chapter in public-private cooperation opened.*

---

* For an in-depth discussion, see Bernard E. Anderson and Isabel V. Sawhill, eds., *Youth Employment and Public Policy* (Englewood Cliffs, N.J.: Prentice-Hall, Inc., 1980).

COMMUNITY ECONOMIC REVITALIZATION

Another field that is spawning innovative examples of cooperation between the public and private sectors in the United States is that of urban economic development. Until well into this century, government's role in the cities was confined to law enforcement and such "housekeeping" services as street and sewer maintenance, water supply, and fire protection. As cities grew more populated and complex, municipal governments took on other responsibilities, such as education, public health, and land use control. For the most part, however, urban life was shaped by private sector actions related to commerce, industry, employment, transportation, and residential construction. An implicit division of responsibilities between business and government was a hallmark of early American urban life.

Nonetheless, the public sector has historically been held responsible for stepping in when things went wrong—as in the early provision of key services like fire protection when the private sector was no longer willing or economically able to provide them. The Great Depression marked a major turning point. With the turnabout by the U.S. Supreme Court that gave the stamp of constitutionality to new federal social and economic programs—the famous "switch in time that saved nine"—the public sector was enabled to treat such pressing problems as unemployment, income security, and housing which previously had been beyond its province. The New Deal ushered in the era of predominance of the federal government in the design and financing of urban-related social programs.

During the 1960s and 1970s, the problems of many of America's cities worsened. Severe economic and social problems cropped up, especially in the Northeast, and were reflected in the erosion of jobs, business investment, and the physical and social environment, accompanied by apparently widening economic disparities and inequities and increasing problems of poverty and racial friction. During the decade of the 1970s, there were marked migrations of population, jobs, and commercial activity away from the Northern Tier states to the South and the West. Northeastern cities were also weakened by metropolitan decentralization of population, business activity, and especially jobs. In short, while social problems tended to increasingly concentrate in central cities, the economic means to combat them was being diluted.

Recent studies by the Rand Corporation, the Urban Institute, and others have shown empirically what many have long known intuitively: that the massive role undertaken by the federal government in urban affairs has indirectly—and inadvertently—contributed to center city decline. During the 1970s, there was some shift in emphasis toward greater responsibility of city governments to solve urban problems: federal revenue-sharing and block grant programs, for example, put the onus on states and cities to identify and prioritize the problems.

For a number of reasons, there is now emerging emphasis on private and public-private actions to revitalize cities. The availability of federal funds to "throw at" urban problems is slowly declining, squeezed between higher public priorities and growing resistance to rising taxes. Second, many city governments, in part because of the decision making thrust on them by federal revenue sharing, are increasingly taking the initiative and generating their own ideas to solve their own problems. Third, faced with the prospect of scarcer federal funds and competition from other geographical areas for jobs and investment, many city governments have sought to unify local political forces while cultivating greater support and involvement from the local business community.

An important factor in the new focus on public-private partnerships is the private sector itself. Forward-looking business leaders have become sharply aware of their stake in solving problems that weaken their host city economically and socially, thereby making it more difficult for their firms to prosper. As a result, private firms in numerous cities across the nation have offered their management and financial expertise to government and to public-private partnership organizations established to improve urban life.

Below are categorized some of the richly varied forms of public sector-private sector cooperation introduced to help invigorate cities.

1. Government Incentives for Business Involvement—Local governments traditionally have provided various kinds of incentives to retain or attract business. Typically these include tax abatements and loan assistance, although a variety of techniques has been tried with mixed success. In recent years state and local governments have increased the use of tax-free municipal bonds to provide financial assistance to business.

- The Industrial Development Agency of New York, created in 1974, issues tax-free revenue bonds to assist industries in the acquisition, construction, and equipping of their facilities.
- Dayton, Ohio's Department of Development provides a number of services to businesses in an attempt to retain businesses located in the city.
- The Urban Development Action Grant program developed by the U.S. Department of Housing and Urban Development assists the private sector, through loans and grants, in such areas as construction, land acquisition, site improvements, development of water or sewer lines, and housing.

2. Government Agencies for Economic Development—Many local governments have separate agencies whose purpose is to provide information and assistance to businesses wishing to locate or expand in their city, to develop coordinated plans for economic development, and to monitor and expedite implementation.

- Milwaukee, Wisconsin's Department of City Development, a line agency of the city government, combines the financial powers of a development corporation, an urban renewal authority, an economic development agency, and a public housing authority.
- Chicago Mayor's Council of Manpower and Economic Advisors, a public policy making body made up of both public and private sector members, directly coordinates manpower, economic development, planning, urban renewal, and housing functions.
- Portland, Oregon's Office of Planning and Development, created by the mayor in 1973, oversees the activities of the planning bureau, the building bureau, the urban renewal authority, and the housing and community development agency.

3. Joint Development Projects—Local governments traditionally have provided basic infrastructure, including streets, water, and sewage, to support private investment. In certain cases, special arrangements are made to accommodate large or otherwise unusual private developments, including public participation in financing and direct public investment in new construction. Several downtown redevelopment efforts have involved the development of coordinated plans of public and private investment.

- Hartford, Connecticut's new Civic Center was cooperatively financed and constructed by the city of Hartford and the Aetna Life and Casualty Company. The land, owned by the city, was acquired through the urban renewal process.
- Nicollet Mall in Minneapolis is a good example of a city government/downtown business partnership. The city was able to finance a special benefits assessment and construct the mall as a regular public works project due to the strong commitment of business leaders.
- Two main renewal projects in downtown Baltimore, Charles Center and Inner Harbor, were planned and executed jointly by the city of Baltimore and the local business community. Local business leaders, through the Charles Center-Inner Harbor Management, Inc., contributed strongly to the management and marketing of the projects, while the city served as master developer.

4. Development Institutions—A variety of quasi-public or limited-profit private organizations have been used to undertake specific development projects or to focus on the redevelopment of certain areas of cities.

- The Philadelphia Industrial Development Corporation, a quasi-public, nonprofit development corporation, was formed in 1958 to stimulate industrial development and retain jobs and tax base in Philadelphia. It has served as a model for urban industrial development corporations throughout the country. Examples of its most recent programs include commercial development financing and market assistance, monitoring of city-sponsored economic development projects, and creation of new financing tools.
- San Diego County's Economic Development Corporation is a nonprofit corporation which interacts with the public through its administration of an industrial attraction and retention program, aimed at creating a highly-skilled business environment. It is primarily concerned with program implementation, as opposed to policy formulation, and attempts to create jobs and diversify employment opportunities for residents of the county.
- The Dayton City-Wide Development Corporation, created in 1972 as a quasi-public, nonprofit real estate development corporation, attempts to stimulate new construction and rehabilitation in the city through the investment approach, rather than through the grant approach. The bulk of the investment the corporation has attracted is in residential facilities and the restoration of historic neighborhoods.

5. Private Spending for Public Purposes—Private companies traditionally have made contributions to support public programs.

- One of the more extensive efforts has been that of a group of businesses in the Minnesota Twin Cities, led by the Dayton Hudson Corporation, to provide 5 percent of profits—which is tax-deductible —for the support of a variety of public programs.
- In Minneapolis, the Downtown Council, a private organization of business leaders, assists in the financing of architectural planning for many public and private projects.
- In cooperation with Chicago's City Planning Department, the Chicago Central Area Committee, a consortium of business leaders, financed the $350,000 Chicago 21 plan to guide development in the central area of Chicago over the next twenty to twenty-five years.

6. Business Expertise Applied to Government—Over the years numerous businesses and businessmen as individuals have responded to the call to work closely with local government to improve its management of public programs. Notable examples include:

- the Economic Development Council of New York City;
- the City Management Advisory Board of the Society for the Promotion, Unification, and Redevelopment of Niagara, Inc., in Niagara Falls, New York; and
- the Committee for Progress in Allegheny County (COMPAC) of Pittsburgh, Pennsylvania.

7. Contracting Public Services to Private Firms—In the last several years there has been growing interest in contracting public services previously provided by government agencies to private businesses. While most city governments contract for many privately produced goods and services, the new interest is in contracting what have generally been thought of as publicly provided services.

- Rural/Metro Fire Department, Inc., provides fire services to the city of Scottsdale, Arizona.
- In Gainesville, Florida, two years ago, the city's sanitation department was abolished and the job of refuse collection was turned over to Houston's Browning-Ferris Industries. As a result, costs have been cut and service complaints reduced.
- The city of Gainesville has also hired Philadelphia's ARA Services to maintain the city's vehicle fleet.

8. Joint Public-Private Promotional Efforts—Chambers of Commerce have traditionally supported local boosterism programs, as have many city governments themselves. While often undertaken individually, they generally are seen by both business and government as serving the same purpose of creating a favorable image for the city in order to attract business and tourism. In some cases, jointly sponsored programs are developed.

- Detroit Renaissance, Inc., a private organization consisting of top executives of Detroit's major businesses, has sponsored a nationwide image program designed to promote the positive features of the city.
- The Port Authority of New York and New Jersey, in addition to its regular operations, carries on world-wide promotional efforts to attract shipping and cargo movement to New York.

9. Government Initiative to Help Solve Business Problems—Occasionally, local political and governmental leaders will take the initiative to help solve private sector problems which affect the local economy.

- The mayor of Jamestown, New York, promoted an effort to establish a productivity improvement program for the ailing manufacturing companies of the Jamestown area.
- The Community and Economic Development Department of Detroit provides business liaison and assistance to firms operating in the city, in an effort to develop, conserve, and promote use of Detroit's land and physical resources.

10. Political Organization and Relationships—One of the least tangible, and yet probably one of the most important, approaches to public-private cooperation is the development of constructive relationships among the various political interests in a community, often through a combination of formal and informal channels.

- In Kansas City, a reform movement which ousted the corrupt Pendergast machine gave rise to a strong, professional city manager style of government and relatively harmonious political relationships between government and the private sector.

11. Improvement of Government Effectiveness in Assisting the Private Sector—One of the most common complaints of businesses is that government bureaucracies are difficult to deal with and have an antibusiness attitude. Some local governments have made conscious efforts to improve the ability and attitude of the various agencies of government that deal with the private sector: cutting red tape, simplifying application and permit procedures, encouraging helpfulness on the part of employees, and the like.

- In Chicago, government administrators and private developers have fostered working relationships that permit detailed problems of development and construction to be resolved with a minimum of red tape.
- The Mayor's Committee for San Francisco, formed after Proposition 13 was adopted in California, includes business, labor, and community leaders working to improve efficiency in city government.

12. Creation of Committees or Task Forces—Business leaders frequently establish committees through their own initiative or at the behest of government, consisting solely of business representatives or in combination with other community representatives, to deal with perceived problems or needs of the community at large. Often these activities extend beyond giving advice and may include corporate actions on jobs, training, plant location, and/or construction.

- In 1977, Mayor Coleman Young commissioned the Economic Growth Council of Detroit, Inc., made up of fifty of the city's leading corporate, labor, and community leaders, to recommend ways in which Detroit's declining economic and fiscal capacity and structural deterioration trends might be halted or reversed.
- Chicago United, organized and supported by the private sector in Chicago, consists of chief executive officers of major businesses who discuss and attempt to deal with such social and economic problems as housing, job training, and economic development.

Community redevelopment efforts sponsored by public-private cooperation received strong support in the late 1970s from the public sector, especially the federal government. In housing policy, for example, the 1970s saw a transition from government owned and operated housing developments for low-income people to an emphasis on subsidies to private developers and apartment owners that would help the same rental groups. The largest federal housing effort, the Section 8 program, epitomized this approach. Although Section 8 was earlier criticized for reducing incentives for new residential construction, President Carter's 1980 budget contained new proposals to remedy that deficiency.

Increasingly, the leveraging of private sector investment is becoming the centerpiece of federal urban policy. The Urban Developing Action Grants program noted above, which was authorized at $400 million per year during 1978-79, requires eligible localities to gain explicit commitments of private funds to qualify for federal funds. The Community Development Block Grants, originally devised by the Nixon Administration and aimed at assisting older, declining cities, can serve to attract additional private investment (although private funds are not required to qualify). A third major federal device to assist local development, loans for housing rehabilitation under Section 312 of the 1964 Housing Act, also can have the effect of stimulating additional private outlays in the most distressed cities. Yet another federal initiative, the experimental Community Economic Development Program (CEDP), was designed to promote partnerships between the private sector and government agencies at the local level to spur revitalization. The ten demonstration cities, assisted by monitoring groups such as the National Council on Urban Economic Development, reported considerable intersector cooperation and, in some cases, the creation of new public-private organizations. CEDP has the potential to catalyze other nongrant localities to set up such public-private efforts.

Throughout the 1970s in particular, the imperatives of urban revitalization gave rise to a remarkable variety of public-private cooperation ventures.

ENERGY CONSERVATION *

In the 1980s, energy may be the successor to urban development and structural unemployment as the big instigator of new working relations between government and business.

Faced as the nation is with the end of cheap and easily available oil, a major task of the 1980s will be to make do with less—or suffer what would appear to be dire consequences. Reducing America's dependence on OPEC oil is likely to be a top priority objective in this decade. Accomplishing this will mean two things: using less energy and developing new sources of supply. In both areas, im-

---

* For further discussion see John C. Sawhill, ed., *Energy Conservation and Public Policy* (Englewood Cliffs, N.J.: Prentice-Hall, Inc., 1979).

proved working relations between business and the public sector can play a key role.

In conservation, the private sector can help a great deal. Business, of course, uses a sizable portion of the nation's energy. Sharply higher energy prices have already provided a powerful incentive to use energy more efficiently, and industry has responded in major measure. Promulgation of information about industry's actions could provide examples for the rest of society to follow.

The private sector can additionally work with government to encourage the public to use less energy. One example is the "energy audit," a low-cost or free service offered by many of the utilities. Trained personnel survey a house or building to isolate spots where energy is "leaking" and where insulation would be most effective. The information enables the property owners to decide whether to invest in energy-saving storm windows, insulation, and the like.

In Rhode Island, public-private cooperation has gone a step further. There business leaders teamed with the state government to put together an organization named Rhode Islanders Saving Energy (RISE). A not-for-profit operation, it provides not only for energy audits upon request but will also handle contracting for, and if necessary financing of, any needed energy-saving installation.

In other activities, such as peak-period pricing of electricity and the promotion of waste recycling for power generation, business support and technology can be enormously helpful. Public-private coordination of carpooling and increased commuter use of mass transit can also have substantial payoffs.

At the municipal level, public-private organizational backing for reduced energy use can be quite effective. During the late 1973 Arab oil embargo, an ad hoc group was formed in Los Angeles to set electricity reduction targets for the city's commercial, industrial, and residential users. Customers were asked by the City Council to cut back to their level of use one year previously or face a 50 percent surcharge on the entire amount of the bill. A city-wide goal of 12 percent reduction in electricity use was set. Much to everyone's surprise, the reduction achieved was 18 percent!

A group of public and private leaders from the Los Angeles community, facing the potential of a blackout, had happened upon

a very effective combination of price and regulation, or what one
authority called:

> a semi-market approach. The program brought dramatic savings with a
> minimum of sacrifice and disruption, and required virtually no invest-
> ment. Two factors made for the program's success. First, a broadly
> based consensus emerged among civic leaders that this plan was the
> fairest and most effective response to a pending crisis. Second, while the
> program set targets, it still possessed a great deal of flexibility and left
> it to consumers to figure out how and where to make their own
> cuts. . . . (*Energy Future,* Robert Stobaugh and Daniel Yergin, eds., New
> York: Random House, 1979, pp. 144–146.)

Public-Private Cooperation on National Objectives?

As the foregoing paragraphs make clear, business and government have demonstrated the ability to work together to help
solve a good many economic and social problems. Covered here are
the examples of unemployment, urban deterioration, and energy
conservation. Other examples can be found in diverse fields such
as improving the educational system, helping fight crime, and improving the effectiveness of health delivery systems—all items certain to be high on America's agenda in the 1980s.

The reader will undoubtedly have recognized, however, that all
these examples are of a preponderantly *local* nature. The cooper-
ating business and government entities are typically conveniently
close together and often well acquainted. Both the problem and
any success in dealing with it can be closely observed and sometimes
even personally experienced.

What about the far more wide-ranging—and often somewhat abstract—challenges posed by the major economic and social problems
that must be faced by this country at the *national* level? Is it possible to marshal private-public sector cooperation on such a scale?
Are any outstanding successes at this level being recorded? Are any
of the cooperative techniques used in successfully attacking local
economic and social problems transferable to the level of national
problems? What is the likelihood of success in that respect?

Perhaps the first national approach that comes to mind is the
federal government's well-known penchant for creating advisory
boards and commissions with members drawn from various parts of
the private sector. Enthusiasm for such organizations has waxed

and waned over the years. Currently it appears at fairly low ebb, if one can reason from the rather strict limits that have been imposed on them. Sometimes permanent and sometimes ad hoc, such advisory groups more often than not have been characterized by lack of authority, lack of conclusiveness, and/or lack of follow-through. While exceptions to one or more of these shortcomings spring to mind—perhaps the Paley Commission on future availability of natural resources and the Kemeny Commission on nuclear safety, for example, deserve that compliment—the track record of this organizational form has not been impressive.

On a pointed national issue, an alternate form of cooperation has recently proved helpful. The Arab boycott of Israel posed very difficult questions for American commerce and demanded legislative treatment to resolve. Private sector leaders from the Business Roundtable and Jewish community groups took the initiative to meet and work out acceptable compromise legislative language. The appropriate government officials were kept apprised, and the resulting language was quickly enacted into law. What had threatened to escalate into a nasty national and international confrontation had been resolved in a workable way.

A quite different form of public-private cooperation also deserves to be mentioned. It is aimed at providing both business and government with more knowledgeable human resources for dealing with national problems. Exemplary of this effort is the President's Executive Exchange Program, which manages the interchange of up-and-coming corporate and government officials for periods of up to one year in responsible work experience.

KEY NATIONAL ECONOMIC AND SOCIAL PROBLEMS

But these kinds of examples tend to pale before the enormity of some of the major economic and social problems clouding America's future. For the purposes of analysis here, it will suffice to mention only nine.

1. Inflation—After more than a decade of episodic but escalating inflation, there are basic questions about the ability of our society to overcome this pernicious addiction. Yet the damage such inflation does to the fabric of both our economic system and our society is so great that it must not be allowed to proceed unchecked. A crucial challenge over the next few years will be to make determined progress toward resolving this problem in ways that are conducive to long-term economic growth and high employment.

2. *Tax Reform*—Dissatisfaction with the tax structure is becoming intense. It is strongly criticized for discouraging efficient economic performance, for proliferating complexities, and for leaving serious inequities unredressed. Yet proposals aimed at ameliorating one or another of these bad effects often would worsen others. A conclusive debate is needed to address the relative priorities that should be assigned to these and other goals, and how and to what extent conflicts between various goals should be resolved.

3. *Fiscal Discipline*—With continued inflationary burdens, taxpayer revolts, pressures for large new spending programs (e.g., for defense and medical care), and simultaneous public dissatisfaction with the performance of many existing government programs, the issue of sharpening methods of fiscal control is likely to move even more into the center of public debate. But which are the best types of control to emphasize? Constitutional or voter-mandated ceilings? Improved legislative and executive branch budget processes? Sharpened governmental management and accountability procedures?

4. *Improving Saving, Capital Investment, Technological Advance, and Productivity*—There is broad agreement that recent U.S. performance in these interrelated areas has been far from satisfactory. There is no such agreement, however, as to why that is so or what are the most important actions that ought to be taken to improve the situation. Yet this unfortunate set of trends, if allowed to continue, can badly damage U.S. international competitiveness, aggravate inflation, and shrink American standards of living.

5. *Energy*—In the United States, important energy problems come in various time dimensions. There are the short-run risks of dealing with OPEC oil price increases and the hazards of abrupt supply cutoffs. There are the medium-term problems of expanding output from present energy sources and using it efficiently. And underneath these is the fundamental long-term problem of managing the transition to renewable sources of energy. Comparative costs, availability, and environmental effects are key considerations in each of these time dimensions.

6. *Regulatory Reform*—The governmental regulations introduced to protect such areas of national concern as the environment, consumer needs, and worker well-being have themselves emerged as major problems. Given the enormous increase in the extent, complexity, and cost of government regulations, pressures for reforms are intensifying. Part of the debate can be expected to revolve around basic questions as to whether particular economic goals can be more effectively achieved through government intervention or through reliance on competitive market processes. In some areas (e.g., nuclear safety) there will be strong demands for a tightening of regulations. In many others, however, the key issue will be how to reduce the scope and rigidity of regulation and to encourage deregulation along the lines recently introduced in the airline industry. Even where some form of government involvement seems indicated, much more attention is likely to be placed on the form that such involvement should take.

7. *Dealing with a More Economically Interdependent World*— World economic interdependence is growing, in many respects so rapidly that it is outpacing the ability of existing national and international institutions to deal with it. If mutual gains from world trade are to be fully realized, there must develop a better common understanding of the rights and obligations of the various participants, big and small, private and public. Furthermore, the United States in particular needs to better adapt its public institutions to the requirements of highly competitive world commerce, in which it is no longer dominant. U.S. regulations, programs, and overseas offices seem more a handicap and less a help to its firms competing internationally than is typical for other industrial nations.

8. *Retirement*—Without significant reforms in the present system, and given projected future changes in inflation rates and demography, the financing of retirement could generate an intolerable burden on future working generations. Accordingly, many public and private studies have already been launched, exploring these and other broad issues that will affect U.S. retirement policies in the coming decades (including social security and other governmental programs as well as private retirement and pension systems). Among the issues that need to be considered are the following.

What should be the relative role and objectives of governmental and private pension programs in the overall retirement system? What role should be preserved for individual discretion and responsibility? What is needed to assure financial soundness of different retirement systems? How should the burden of changing demographic trends on retirement systems be shared among generations?

9. *Changing Concepts of Work*—The combination of changes in the demographics of population and the labor force, worker attitudes, and the skill requirements of advancing technology will impel major alterations in the concepts and standards of work. Major issues include how increased options can be created for greater flexibility in work time, work sites, and job design, and how the time and energies of individuals can best be allocated among work, education, volunteer activities, and leisure throughout their lifetimes. But such alterations will be difficult to achieve because the definitions of work are deeply embedded in law, business and union practices, and personal ethics. Furthermore, it will be vitally important that such work changes not leave a sizable body of involuntarily unemployed.

These are extraordinarily difficult problems. In contrast to the typically *operational* nature of numerous problems cited earlier that business and government are attacking cooperatively, these are better termed *strategic* problems. They demand the resolution of conflicting objectives and priorities over relatively long time horizons. Economic, political, and social considerations are very much intertwined in them. Moreover, these problems must be handled with recognition of the growing interdependence of nations. Actions that might once have been regarded as an acceptable solution to a problem in our country are now inhibited by the potential for some offsetting foreign response.

MORE CENTRALIZED ECONOMIC PLANNING?

In the minds of some observers, strategic problems of this complexity can only be resolved by moving to more centralized economic planning. As proponents see it, only by providing a centralized entity to make or influence key economic decisions can the important nonmarket and social aspects of these problems be adequately taken into account. Nonmarket and social considerations range all the way from equitable distribution of income to environmental protection to national security. Advocates envision that business, labor, and other views on these questions can be appropriately taken into account by including them in some way in the planning process. It is felt in some quarters that centralized planning decisions have the potential to provide relatively clear, definitive, and long-lived decisions on key issues on which subsequent private decision making can depend. With uncertainties thus reduced, it is thought that private economic activities could proceed more confidently.

Without entering into a detailed analysis of the pros and cons of centralized economic planning, it can be noted that experience has produced some discouraging results. Liberal industrial democracies of Western Europe have found that a key deficiency of simple planning targets is that they do not deal with the equity problem. Overall planning for production, investment, and the like does not assure that the proceeds will be distributed equitably. European experience suggests that the position of most disadvantaged citizens may not measurably improve, at least in relative terms.

There are other observed difficulties with centralized planning in market democracies. It typically gives rise to delays and rigidities. The timing of changes in the plan being arbitrary can add to uncertainty. The plan often leads to reduced efficiency and economic growth. The setting of growth targets, whether in private consumption and incomes or in collective consumption, often does not take account of unanticipated adverse side effects such as pollution, noise, social dissatisfaction, or urban crowding. Moreover, planning cannot promptly take into consideration extraordinary events such as massive oil price increases, unforeseen distortions caused by economic interdependence, or the effects of floating exchange rates.

The Western Europeans' response to these difficulties has been to become significantly more flexible in collective target setting. By the 1970s, planning in Western Europe had evolved into a more amorphous mechanism chiefly creating a climate for certain desired activities such as investment in research and development and pollution control. Tax incentives and public grants have been instituted to compensate for regional or industrial imbalances in investment and employment. Other compensatory measures have included greater worker participation in industry management decisions and gradual decentralization and reform of institutions to allow for regional differences.

The Japanese experience with planning is riskier to try to draw lessons from, because it is hard to tell how much it is dependent upon cultural relationships absent in the United States. One can use the reverse approach, however, looking for characteristics and developments in the American economic system that might be built upon to help deal with some of the major economic and social problems that are elsewhere attacked through more centralized planning modes.

AN ALTERNATIVE: ANTICIPATORY ANALYSIS

A key attribute of the American economic system has been its adaptability to changing circumstances. For a variety of reasons, a growing number of corporations and thought centers are now looking further ahead than before to identify emerging issues. Partly this may be because the most troublesome economic problems in sight seem to take longer to prepare for and longer to resolve.

In any event, the opportunity exists to try to push forward this kind of endeavor in *early issue recognition*, in ways that could involve a great deal of public and private sector interaction. Thought leaders such as major research institutes, centers for corporate executive cogitation, the Council of Economic Advisers, and the Joint Economic Committee could try harder to spotlight approaching major economic problems (the 1979 reports of both these latter two entities were significant steps forward in this respect).

Once a major emerging issue is recognized, *fact-finding and analysis* are the next steps. Scholars would need to become more involved in this exercise, and they would need to be both encouraged and supported to do so.

The resulting welter of issues, facts, and judgments would need to be winnowed. This is a task for organizations specializing in *research evaluation and consensus-building*—of which I count the CED to be one.

If, and as, identified issues and their relevant information assume manageable proportions, *dialogue* would be the natural next step—congressional hearings, presidential commissions, university symposia, corporate conferences, and public meetings of various sorts.

If, happily, some final *consensus* emerges as to what to do about the issue, it could be published in books, declared in presidential messages, and enshrined in law. In the American economic system, however, the most important result would be the spreading total of individual actions taken by decision makers in all walks of business in the light of this clearer knowledge. Our society has organizations and institutions adept at *disseminating such knowledge* and spurring action based on it.

The system that has been outlined in the preceding five brief paragraphs would provide abundant opportunities for public and private sector interchange. It is, of course, a messy system. Under it, many issues would receive some undeserved attention, and some very important issues would not be recognized, correctly analyzed, or carried to sustainable consensus on the first try. The answer, in this system, would be to try again. This system would work best if we could manage to recognize and work hardest on the really major emerging problems that threaten all or large parts of our society. Conferences such as that sponsored by The American Assembly on "Economic Issues of the Presidency: 1980 and Beyond" could be an important help in identifying such high-priority problems.

This might be termed a system of *anticipatory analysis*, as distinct from a scheme of centralized planning. What would make it pull together are not laws or regulations, but the convincing powers of argument and analysis. It would seem to blend well with American traditions of pluralism, open communication, compromise, and pragmatic accommodation to major social and economic forces.

A business could do its own anticipatory analysis, or it could participate as much in developing a national consensus analysis as its own intellectual resources warranted. The same would be true of every other institutional source of ideas and analysis. The long-run nature of most major issues would attract chiefly the more foresighted private and public leaders. Indeed, the span of issue resolution might often exceed the term of office for both the average elected politician and the average corporate chief executive officer. Furthermore, the participants will probably have to be responsive to the public's increased inclination to question the fairness and reasonableness of economic analysis and decisions.

For those private sector leaders who can adapt to these conditions, however, this system may provide a way to cooperate with the public sector, amicably and to the full extent of their abilities, in analyzing and dealing with the major national economic problems that arise to plague our country. In turn, the President who can evoke this kind of participation by talented leaders of the private sector will have done much to help meet the challenge of the 1980s.

David L. Grove

5

The Changing International Role of the United States

Introduction

At the close of World War II, the United States found itself in a position of international military, political, and economic dominance which would enable it, if it so chose, to have an enormous influence on the future course of world events. The United States chose to seize this opportunity. Its political leaders had a vision of the sort of postwar world they wanted to achieve and of the institutions and policies needed to make their vision come to pass. And, by the standards that are relevant and reasonable in such matters, the vision can be said to have largely materialized in the first decade after the war.

At the same time, it has to be recognized that the environment

DAVID L. GROVE *is president of the United States Council of the International Chamber of Commerce, Inc. and senior economic advisor of the Marine Midland Bank. Previously, he was corporate vice president and chief economist of IBM. Dr. Grove has served on a number of U.S. government advisory groups and as an advisor to central banks in several foreign countries. He is a trustee of the Committee for Economic Development and director of several other organizations and companies. He also is a member of* Time Magazine's *board of economists.*

at the end of World War II, and the U.S. policies which grew out of that environment, could not be expected to last forever. In fact, success in carrying out the early postwar vision would in itself fundamentally change the environment and, consequently, the appropriateness of the corresponding policies. Major historical changes take time, however, and it is not always easy immediately to determine how powerful emerging forces are and where they eventually will lead. Nonetheless, enough evidence has accumulated to provide grounds for concluding that the world now already has demonstrably entered a major new phase in international affairs, a phase which is creating a new set of basic problems and challenges for U.S. policy makers. At the same time, it also is fair to say that this country's leaders (not just government officials but intellectual and business leaders as well) have not yet been able to form a new and integrated vision of either the nature of the challenges or of how this country should deal with them.

The Changed International Environment

International economic policies perforce must reflect and respond to the environment in which they operate. Before discussing policy issues, therefore, one should first describe one's perception of the environment.

The late 1960s marked the end of a major era which spanned roughly the first two postwar decades. In that period, the dominant political and economic forces in the world were largely harmonious and supportive to international economic growth and cooperation. Now, the world is entering a new era in which the fundamental forces are becoming less harmonious, with disturbing crosscurrents which will impede economic growth and international cooperation.

What were the fundamental forces which dominated the period from the end of World War II to the end of the 1960s and made it possible for the free world to enjoy unprecedented economic growth and rapid expansion in international trade and investment?

Clearly, a brief review cannot do justice to exceptions and qualifications; nonetheless, it can help to bring matters into sharp focus and provide a correct perspective of the problems and challenges ahead. Accordingly, let us outline the dominant features of roughly the first two decades following World War II. There are six such features which seem to be of particular importance for any analysis of the *current* situation.

1. The United States clearly was the dominant military power during that period. We provided a military umbrella for Europe and Japan and thereby made it possible for those countries to devote their resources almost exclusively to raising their productivity and standard of living. This situation also strengthened the motivation of other countries to follow the U.S. leadership, both in political and economic affairs. Russia, the only possible military threat to major American interests in Europe, entered the period in greatly weakened condition and regained its strength only after a number of years. In the Far East, China, too, was weak and in no position to fight a major war. Germany and Japan no longer had any military power.

2. Particularly in the first half of the period, the United States subordinated its economic policies to its international political objectives. Those objectives were to help Europe and Japan restore their war-shattered economies and to become strong, vigorous allies of this country as a counterweight to the inevitable revival of Russian (and possibly Chinese) power. This explains the Marshall Plan and the equanimity with which we watched the decline in our share both of world exports of manufactured goods and of the world's international monetary reserves. Unlike Great Britain in the nineteenth century, the U.S. government did not use its political and military dominance to promote our exports and obtain imports at minimum cost. Quite the contrary, we were willing to let our relative economic position weaken in order to promote our broad political objectives. We perceived this to be in our own as well as the world's best interests. We believed that rapid postwar recovery in the industrial nations and rapid economic growth in the developing nations would make the world more stable and a stronger bulwark against Soviet Russia and its satellites.

3. The United Nations was created to help preserve world peace.

4. A new international financial system—the Bretton Woods System—was established. It was designed to promote international monetary order and stability and to provide international finance for economic growth. It had two major institutions to implement the system: the International Monetary Fund (IMF) and the World Bank. In each of these, the United States had a preponderance of

influence. The International Monetary Fund was to preside over a new international monetary system by administering a set of rules of the game governing exchange rates and by providing short-term balance of payments loans to countries needing such assistance. In this new monetary system the U.S. dollar was established as the pivot around which other currencies would revolve. It was thought that, with this system, the world could largely avoid the competitive depreciations, exchange controls, and other disruptive trade and monetary practices which had created serious international tensions in the 1930s.

The second pillar of the Bretton Woods System was the International Bank for Reconstruction and Development—commonly called "the World Bank." Its purpose was to provide long-term financing for sound economic growth.

5. To promote international trade by multilateral agreements which would lower tariffs, quotas, and other types of trade barriers, another international organization, the International Trade Organization (ITO), was designed. The ITO was to prescribe rules of the game to govern international trade, thus paralleling the work of the IMF in the monetary sphere. Although the ITO never came into being because of opposition in the United States, its objectives of progress toward trade liberalization were embodied in the General Agreement on Tariffs and Trade (GATT).

6. Less formally, but no less importantly, most countries embraced so-called Keynesian domestic economic policies which, it was widely believed, would enable them to tame the business cycle and achieve high levels of economic growth and employment and to do so within a framework of a reasonable degree of overall price stability and balance of payments equilibrium. Of course, even then, it was recognized that Keynesian policies could be highly inflationary if pushed to excess, but it was thought that such excesses could be avoided, for the most part, especially if the IMF was vigilant in the discharge of its responsibilities.

Thus, between 1944 and 1948 there emerged a harmonious overall conceptual framework, or design, and a set of institutions to make the postwar political and economic system work. It was an impressive and inspiring design, closely modeled along the lines that Woodrow Wilson had tried but failed to establish at the end of World War I. It was a great tribute to his vision.

Perhaps most important of all, this time there was an almost universal optimism that, even allowing for the frailties of political leaders, the system would work.

Of course, the era was not without its problems and challenges. There were the "Cold War," incidents over Berlin, the Korean War, the Cuban missile crisis, and the turmoil that often surrounded the passage of colonies to independent sovereignty. Nevertheless, the problems did not then seem to be structural or beyond the capability of the institutional arrangements that had been established.

By and large, the system certainly did perform quite well over most of the two-decade period. Europe and Japan were reconstructed quickly and continued to grow at a record pace. The less-developed countries grew even faster. And those that were colonies at the beginning of the period—and there were many of them—achieved their independence. Witness how few colonies remain today.

The international monetary system served the world quite satisfactorily for a number of years. International trade and investment thrived. Barriers to trade and investment shrank substantially. Research and development outlays, along with technological progress, advanced with rapid strides and provided the basis for entire new industries, with their concomitant investment and employment opportunities.

The real cost of energy declined significantly during this period. In the United States, for example, the real wholesale price of energy dropped roughly a third between 1948 and 1968. The declining cost of energy promoted industrialization everywhere. It also promoted rapid expansion of markets for automobiles, other consumer durable goods, and housing.

Given these developments, little wonder that advances in labor productivity moved well above their earlier trend lines. High domestic rates of growth made it much easier for countries everywhere to cope with internal pressures for social progress. Radicalism, and especially demands for redistribution of wealth, generally do not get very far very fast so long as the poor see the size of the total national pie expanding rapidly and can experience a good increase in the serving on their plate year by year. Moreover, strong growth holds out the promise that their children's lot will be much better than theirs. And, finally, those who are very well off generally are somewhat less resistant to reforms when their own incomes are growing substantially; in nearly all countries this was the situation most of the time during that period.

The developing countries, while continuously endeavoring to extract more aid from the developed countries, as is their normal pattern, by and large cooperated with the system—or at least did not try very hard to upset it. In any event, they hardly had the economic or political strength to affect the system in a major way. And a number of them were preoccupied with their own internal problems as they moved from the status of colonies to that of independent nations. Capital flowed to the developing countries in rather large amounts: from new international lending institutions such as the World Bank and its affiliates, from governments of the developed countries in the form of bilateral aid, and from private business sources. These capital inflows financed a substantial amount of economic development. Here again, growth in the size of the total pie muted the contest for relative shares; in this case, the contest between the developed and the underdeveloped parts of the world.

In short, the first two postwar decades were a "golden era" in many ways (although they did not always seem so at the time). There was a general faith in the ability of authorities and institutions, both nationally and internationally, to deal with age-old economic problems of poverty and wealth and thereby brighten the outlook for peace and stability. It was an era which invited and promoted international enterprises and the spread of their technological and managerial know-how.

Then, as the 1960s neared their end, and even more so in the past decade, the system increasingly began to display signs of stress and fracture.

The United States lost the military dominance it once had; that dominance began to decline once the United States no longer was the sole possessor of nuclear bombs and as Russia recovered from the devastation of the war and embarked on a program of large-scale military spending. Now our relative military power has shrunk to a level such that our ability to protect our allies has been questioned—most cogently by Henry Kissinger in a speech in Brussels in the fall of 1979 which attracted much attention. In addition, the experience of the United States in Vietnam not only weakened our military reputation, it also undermined our image of moral leadership in many circles abroad (as well as at home).

Similarly, the leadership of the United States in international monetary affairs crumbled. The Bretton Woods monetary system broke down, perhaps in large measure because of excessive creation of dollars by our monetary authorities, but also because some other countries were unwilling to let their currencies appreciate sufficiently when they became grossly undervalued. In addition, the system contained no mechanism by which the United States could initiate a devaluation of the dollar whenever the dollar became fundamentally overvalued, which was the case in the late 1960s. In 1971, we severed the official parity between the dollar and gold and, in effect, brought the Bretton Woods System to a formal end. By the end of 1973, the world had been forced onto a so-called floating exchange rate system, in the absence of any acceptable alternatives, since there appeared to be no chance of returning to the Bretton Woods System. However, it really is a "managed" rather than a freely floating system, though it has no objective or formal mechanism for determining the appropriate level toward which a currency's float will be "managed." The system sometimes is more accurately described as a system of "dirty floating" because there is no internationally agreed upon set of rules governing exchange market interventions by the national monetary authorities; therefore, it is easier for countries to manipulate their exchange rate for their own national interests and harder to call them to account for failure to give adequate weight to adverse effects on other countries. In many ways, therefore, the current system is more of a nonsystem than a system.

Although there were a few eruptions of inflation in the United States during the period between the end of World War II and 1967, the period as a whole was characterized by very moderate upward drift in the general price level. A new round of inflation was experienced in 1968-70, largely as a consequence of the inflationary fiscal policy employed in the Johnson administration in financing the Vietnam War. In addition, many of the social and economic policies adopted in the earlier postwar years had a latent inflationary potential which was beginning to come to the surface by the end of the 1960s. Although the rate of inflation receded in

1971 and 1972, it surged upward in 1973, partly in response to a sharp rise in OPEC oil prices. Pressures from the cost side were strengthened by the expansionary monetary and fiscal policies pursued as the country emerged from the 1974 recession. The combined effect of these forces was to drive inflation to new highs. Since then, frequent further jumps in oil prices have maintained the pressure on producer costs, while monetary and fiscal policy has done little to restrain growth in aggregate demand for goods and services. Worse still, expectations of persistent high rates of inflation now have become deeply rooted in the public's mind and show no signs of being eradicable by anything short of a depression of intolerable severity. Thus, we currently not only have the disease of inflation, we also seem to have no acceptable cure—at least in the short term. The inability of the United States to bring inflation under control, and the related inability to strengthen the dollar, have diminished other countries' respect for us and our policies in nearly all areas of economic policy.

The United States' great dependency on oil imports (even though relatively far smaller than that of most other industrial nations) and its seeming inability to deal with this vulnerability have further contributed to the perception of loss of our international leadership, as has the growing dependency of the dollar on the portfolio decisions of OPEC money managers.

There is another aspect of America's postwar international role that needs to be mentioned, even though it may be more psychological than fundamental. Presidents Roosevelt, Truman, Eisenhower, and Kennedy each were viewed as men with a keen interest in foreign affairs and were accepted in most of the rest of the world as leaders with a truly international vision. This perception of these presidents made America's foreign leadership easier to exercise. There was, however, quite a different foreign reaction to President Johnson, his objectives, and his policies. While President Nixon succeeded in regaining some of the respect abroad that President Johnson had lost, the recovery was far from complete, and foreign attitudes about him and his policies were quite mixed. President Ford was regarded as less interested in providing world leadership than was his immediate predecessor. And President Carter has been a source of much puzzlement to foreigners and to their national leaders. Among the essential conditions for any improvement in the leadership role of the United States may well be not only the forging of a constructive and consistent set of international political and economic policies by the United States, but also an ability by the President himself to inspire foreign understanding and acceptance of them. This is no small challenge.

What are likely to be the major consequences of a continuation in the decline in America's capacity to provide firm political and economic leadership? One is a greater risk that festering economic, political, and military problems may spread and not be resolved before they have done considerable harm. It will be harder to obtain international cooperation, especially in difficult circumstances requiring sacrifices by some. The United States no longer has the leverage it once had to assure cooperation, and, as a consequence, other countries have less compulsion to submerge their perceived self-interests to the common international welfare. This is not to suggest that international cooperation is ending—it is not. But it is to suggest that much of the high degree of international cooperation which marked the first two postwar decades was a reflection of a sort of "Pax Americana" that now is withering away and leaving a power vacuum in the process. This does not augur well for the handling of world problems and crises. International power vacuums, throughout history, have been a great source of instability.

Another discernible change that has occurred in the world environment has been the shift from a rapid economic growth trend to a substantially slower one. This process seems to be occurring in nearly all countries, apart from the oil-exporting ones. There are several explanations as to why it is occurring.

One is that sharp rises in the cost of energy have been and will continue to be a key retardant to economic growth, both because of their direct effects and because of their role in driving up prices generally. OPEC producers may be able to continue to price aggressively because there are the rather dim prospects of any substantial growth in supplies of nonoil sources of energy within the current decade. Quite apart from the depressing effects of high energy costs, therefore, there is the prospect that limited supplies of energy, even without any dramatic interruptions in the flow of oil, will act as a strong brake on world-wide economic growth in the 1980s.

Another view that sometimes is heard is that advances in knowledge come in long waves, and that the first two postwar decades witnessed a "second industrial revolution" based on an accumulation of science-based technologies which now are being rather fully explored. According to this view, it will take some time before the reservoir of new knowledge becomes full again, which then would provide a wellspring for the next wave of growth. Still another and very closely related thesis is that of the late Professor Joseph A. Schumpeter, one of the greatest students of capitalism and economic growth. Schumpeter made a sharp distinction between "invention" and the introduction of invention into the marketplace—which he calls "innovation." He maintained that while inventions may possibly be more or less evenly spaced throughout history, their rate of adoption, or "innovation," in capitalist societies is not. Innovations, he said, usually have come in great waves, as the original advance spreads and becomes widely adopted. The center point of his view of the history of capitalism is the role of the entrepreneur in this process of pushing aside the old and introducing the new, in what Schumpeter called a "gale of creative destruction." Profits are the reward for innovation and the related risk-taking in his scheme of things.

According to those who accept his thesis and apply it to the current situation, the world has just finished one major wave, and it will take some time before another will start. The most likely candidate would seem to be a wave driven by energy-saving and energy-creating investment. An appropriate question, however, is whether the prevailing world-wide climate of government regulation will delay or dampen the inception and strength of such a wave because the prospective profits may be kept to levels which are not proportionate to the risks that would be involved in early and vigorous efforts to accelerate their introduction

Whatever the causes may be, what are the consequences of the immediate prospect of slower growth in output everywhere? Clearly, the foremost problem will be that of distribution of income and wealth, both within countries and also internationally. The struggle for a "share" of the domestic national incomes and of the global international income is likely to become more intense and often bitter. This likelihood is enhanced by the higher level of expectations which years of rapid growth have produced, both in the developing and the industrially advanced parts of the world. Higher unemployment rates will tend to lead to greater demands for an expansion of government's role in economic affairs at the same time that public confidence in government's ability to manage economic affairs, and to solve social problems, has eroded. The opportunities this environment will create for demagoguery are obvious! It also will create conditions favorable for trade protectionism and economic nationalism generally.

The so-called "North-South dialogue," that is, the struggle by the poorer developing nations to achieve what they call "the new international economic order," is likely to become more acrimonious, especially as the higher prices of imported energy seriously jeopardize their rates of growth and their ability to service their mounting foreign debt. This will not be a situation conducive to high rates of investment in those countries by international firms or even by their own indigenous firms. Neither will it provide an inviting prospect for international lenders. It will, however, provide fertile soil for extremist ideologies to sprout and spread in the poorer parts of the world.

Nonetheless, the global outlook offers some favorable possibilities that should not be overlooked. It should be emphasized that they are possibilities, not necessarily probabilities. Whether they come to pass will depend largely on the degree of enlightened leadership provided here and abroad.

One of these possibilities, in the industrialized countries, is that governments may awaken to the need to stimulate research and development expenditures and business investment to a greater extent than heretofore. One already sees some promising signs in this country that public and official attitudes in this regard may be changing.

In the United States, there is some evidence which suggests that more attention is being given to the need to stimulate domestic business investment and, in other ways as well (such as through reducing the drag of government regulation and through improvements in our educational system), to provide a foundation for raising the rate of productivity growth. Failure to make progress in this direction will make the continued long-term decline of the value of the dollar both internationally and domestically a near certainty.

Still another potentially favorable development in the United States is that efforts to pursue monetary and fiscal policies designed to curb inflation may be more serious than they have been. Prudent monetary and fiscal policies now would permit faster economic growth later, as well as greater international competitiveness of American manufactured goods. Among other things, a lower rate of inflation would increase the willingness of American businessmen to invest in plant and equipment in this country because it would reduce uncertainty. Often overlooked is that a high average rate of inflation invariably is accompanied by a wider spread of *individual* price movements about the average level, and businessmen typically base their physical investment decisions on their expectations about *specific relative* prices and costs rather than on their expectations about the price level as a whole. A lower rate of inflation also would strengthen the attractiveness of the dollar as an acceptable vehicle for domestic and international *financial* investment.

Another noteworthy major change in the environment pertains to the early postwar conventional wisdom about governments' ability to manage their domestic economies. As was stated earlier, in the first two postwar decades there was a widespread "Keynesian" notion that governments could manage aggregate demand and that, by so doing, they could assure orderly economic growth. It also generally was believed that such growth would enable governments to resolve other vexing social problems, to a large extent. The problems of the poor were viewed as being almost exclusively problems of lack of jobs and money. "Keynesian" fiscal policies, therefore, could solve them.

That view has turned out to be naive (perhaps in part, oddly enough, due to their initial success which created a new set of expectations and conditions that then proceeded to undermine the efficacy of such policies). Attempts to sustain aggregate demand now increasingly seem to cause more inflation rather than raise output and employment, and attempts to curb demand in the short run seem to curb mainly output and employment while exerting relatively little and only belated restraint on wages and prices. And most major social problems—including unemployment—have turned out to be far more complex than had been imagined. All too often the earlier conventional hypotheses about their causes and cures have not held up, and no new hypotheses have commanded wide acceptance as yet. But two things certainly now seem evident. First, it is much harder to maintain high levels of real income and employment than had been imagined, and, second, the major social problems have roots which run far deeper than just a lack of jobs and money—though availability of adequate employment opportunities remains a critical requirement that should not be overlooked.

In one sense, this new and more realistic perception of problems is, in itself, a part of the current dilemma of policy makers because there no longer is a credible theoretical foundation on which to build government economic policies. But in another sense it offers a great opportunity. It offers an opportunity because it means that the major thrust of economic and social policy over the next couple of decades, whatever it may turn out to be, now is in its early stage of formulation.

Before proceeding to a discussion of the implications of all of the foregoing for U.S. international economic policy, it may be helpful to summarize the points that need to be kept in mind.

1. The distribution of international military, political, and economic power has changed markedly, leaving the United States much more heavily dependent on the cooperation of other countries, both developed and underdeveloped. As a corollary, other countries are less dependent on us.

2. There has been a fragmentation of the international political system. This has been both a result of the reduced dependency of other nations on the United States and a contributing factor to their becoming more independent. The movement of a large number of former colonies to full sovereign status has increased this fragmentation and has, in a number of ways, been a destabilizing force.

3. As a consequence of the increased independence and fragmentation, other countries now tend to be considerably more aggressive about asserting their own perceived self-interests and feel under much less compulsion to follow the United States' perception of what is in the noncommunist world's best interest.

4. The OPEC nations have emerged as an entirely new and powerful force in the world economy, to the great disadvantage of the United States, which thus far has been unable to reduce its

heavy dependence on oil imports from OPEC countries and to find a solution to the disruptive effects OPEC surpluses are having on the international position of the dollar. Neither do we seem able to do much to help reduce other countries' dependence on OPEC, and this erodes our influence with them in a number of ways.

5. The United States also has become heavily dependent on foreign sources of supply of many critical materials other than oil. Some of those materials come mainly from developing countries with unstable governments; therefore, those sources must be regarded as quite unreliable. Moreover, prospects for uninterrupted long-term availability of oil from the Middle East are not reassuring. First, there is the political instability of the area. In addition, the Russian invasion of Afghanistan, combined with the likelihood that Russia's growing needs for energy may soon outstrip that country's domestic production, raise further doubts about the dependability of our oil supplies from much of the Middle East.

6. In the past decade, the United States has been experiencing very low rates of productivity growth. While it was to be expected that Europe and Japan would outstrip the United States in productivity growth during the postwar years of reconstruction and modernization of their industrial facilities, the gap between their rates and ours has remained disturbingly large, and this situation seems likely to persist.

7. The low rates of productivity growth, the large oil-related trade deficits, and the seemingly intractable inflation problem all are combining to undermine the position of the United States: (a) as a *net* supplier of capital to the rest of the world, (b) as an effective competitor in manufactured goods, and (c) as a stable source of the rest of the world's international liquidity and international means of payment.

8. Largely because of the enormous increases in imported oil costs and because of efforts by governments everywhere to curb the rise in their overall price levels, the world faces at least several years of below-normal rates of growth of economic activity. In many countries this will create domestic social tensions which will lead their governments to adopt economic policies of a nationalist and protectionist stripe. These policies, in turn, will tend to hurt other countries and will create serious international tensions.

9. The elaborate complex of international institutions established between 1944 and 1948 seems to be having great difficulty in dealing effectively with the major political and economic problems now surfacing. Moreover, the international political and economic complexities are such that it is not clear how these institutions can be strengthened in presently prevailing circumstances.

Economic Policy Implications for the United States

The changed environment has created or intensified a number of economic issues and consequences which the United States must face. It may be well to make a list of some of the most obvious ones and to comment on each very briefly.

1. The growth in protectionism abroad will be adverse for American exports. Moreover, protectionism increasingly is applying to trade in services as well as to trade in goods. The trend toward extending protectionism to trade in services is likely to accelerate and be significantly harmful to our total trade position because American companies have been effective innovators and highly effective international competitors in the service area. The United States needs to play a strong and active role both in the GATT and in bilateral negotiations to moderate the drift toward protectionism. In particular, we need to assure that the constructive potential of the recent "Tokyo Round" of the Multilateral Trade Negotiations conducted under GATT auspices is fully realized. At the same time, the United States must avoid actions of its own which can properly be viewed by others as "not practicing what we preach."

2. The rapid technological advances and innovations abroad appear to have made some American industries—or at least parts of some industries—noncompetitive. Should our government adopt the Japanese policy toward "sunset" industries—that is, actively encourage their phasing out—or should it succumb to pleas for financial assistance and protection? In the United States, a "sunset" policy probably could not be as forceful as it is in Japan because of the different character of the government-business relationship, but it could take the form of a policy of firm denial of all requests for financial assistance, for tariff and quota protection, and for other kinds of government action on behalf of "sunset"

companies and industries. In the more turbulent and unsettled conditions which seem likely to characterize the 1980s, should national security considerations be given more weight in shielding industries weakened by imports? If so, what guidelines should be adopted to minimize economic inefficiency?

Clearly, our ability to persuade other countries to eschew protectionism adverse to us will be enhanced if we minimize our own exceptions to free trade principles, of which there are not a few. On the other hand, the slow rate of economic growth this country seems likely to experience during the next few years will increase the number of ailing companies and demands for assistance, including greater protection from import competition.

The one thing that most certainly needs to be done is to continue to explore the extent to which needless or unnecessarily burdensome U.S. government regulations are contributing to the inability of American companies and industries to compete with foreigners. Another issue is the extent to which our tax structure impedes research, development, and investment expenditures by American businesses; in fact, given the new environment and outlook, it would seem appropriate to adopt tax policies which actively promote investment and innovation and, correspondingly, the supply of savings. Similarly, in the absence of international agreement on the credit terms exporters may offer, the United States would seem to need to provide our exporters with financing capabilities comparable to those available to our foreign competitors. Apparently, this is not the situation now.

3. The government should decide what its position really should be with respect to foreign direct investment by American firms. Attitudes about such investment have been quite ambivalent. On the one hand, at times there have been allegations that American direct investment overseas has resulted in less investment here at home. It also has been charged that the present method of taxing foreign-source income tends to make it more profitable, after taxes, for an American firm to locate production facilities abroad in instances in which prospective *pretax* rates of return at the foreign location are no higher than they would be at a U.S. location. On the other hand, a number of studies have reported that tax considerations seldom are an important determinant of foreign investment decisions; the primary consideration is that a foreign

manufacturing facility is the only way a company can maintain and expand its foreign market position. Thus, in most cases, there is not a choice between serving the foreign market from U.S. facilities and from overseas facilities; rather, it is a choice between serving it from an overseas location or losing ground to foreign competitors.

The real issue is the following: to what extent is it important to the global political and economic position of the United States to have American business have a substantial presence all over the world? If the answer is that it is quite important, then American business abroad should be given tax treatment on foreign earnings which is no more onerous than that borne by foreign business firms; otherwise, American firms will be at a competitive disadvantage.

Sometimes this issue is posed in terms of whether American direct investment abroad makes a net positive contribution to our balance of payments position. Posing the issue only in this way is not satisfactory. First, it views the issue too narrowly, especially at a time when the overall international political and economic position of the United States has been eroding. Second, it is impossible to answer the question definitively by econometric and other statistical techniques because these cannot predict what would have happened to American exports and imports in the absence of such investment over an extended period of time. As a matter of record, however, most carefully prepared studies have concluded that, on balance, American direct investment does contribute positively to our balance of payments. In relatively few cases, these studies report, is the American market supplied from the parent's foreign facilities, and where it is, the U.S. market probably would otherwise be won by foreign exporters.

Another aspect of the direct investment issue deserves special attention. As already noted, the United States increasingly is becoming dependent on foreign sources of supplies of minerals and other raw materials, and global competition for supplies of some such materials will become even greater in the decade of the 1980s. Can American economic and security needs best be served by encouraging American firms to invest in the overseas development and production of these products or should the field, by lack of official encouragement, be left largely to others? If the answer favors active American involvement, what are the most effective measures to support the objective?

In this connection, it should be recognized, of course, that American-owned facilities would be vulnerable to disruptions occasioned by political instability. But, to the extent that such investment led to greater development of potential sources of supply abroad than would otherwise have occurred, the world-wide supply situation would be eased. Moreover, it would provide insurance against possible purchase arrangements by others which effectively might block our buyers from access to some foreign supplies.

4. What should the international role of the dollar be, and how can it best be achieved? It is clear that the post-World War II enthronement of the dollar at Bretton Woods in 1944 was a passing phenomenon whose time is running out. It also is clear that no other national currency is capable of taking its place; neither does any other sovereign government seek to assume the role of the United States in this regard. Yet, unless some solution is found to the present unsettled and unsatisfactory situation, growth of world trade and investment will be constrained and international financial panic will remain a hovering spectre. Moreover, there is a risk that existing currency blocs will become stronger and more inward looking and that new ones will be formed. This is the stuff that breeds economic nationalism and trade protectionism.

Because so much depends on the outcome, therefore, international currency reform and how the transition to a new and more stable system can best be managed deserve high priority on the administration's list of policy issues. Success in this direction, however, in large measure will depend on credible prior U.S. actions to improve this nation's domestic economic performance and to enhance foreign understanding and acceptance of our foreign policy objectives. In short, the problem is closely related to the need to restore world confidence in America's leadership in world affairs generally.

5. Should the United States actively promote the establishment of a new international financial facility of large enough scale to provide an effective and stable mechanism for recycling OPEC surpluses? To be successful, such an international facility would have to offer sufficiently attractive terms to OPEC nations to induce them to accept the obligations of the facility as the best ve-

hicle for their surpluses. The facility would have to be capable of financing much of the oil deficits of the developing countries, and, at times, of some of the developed countries as well. Such a facility might be managed by the International Monetary Fund as a separate entity, with its own structure of member voting rights.

The IMF's present resources and lending requirements are inadequate for long-term financing of oil deficits. Moreover, the present voting structure in the fund would be incompatible with acceptance by the OPEC nations of a commitment to deposit much of their financial surpluses there.

A number of technical and political problems would have to be addressed. But the need to provide a more stable recycling mechanism is urgent because it is unlikely that American commercial banks can safely continue recycling OPEC funds to the developing countries at the high rates of the past several years—nor can European and Japanese banks.

6. Not unrelated to the preceding issue is the matter of so-called Euro-currency markets and their role. Are they a risk to international financial and economic stability, or do they provide an effective form of international intermediation? Do these transactions really seriously hamper the monetary policy of the Federal Reserve System and of other central banks, or are they a safety valve against misguided monetary policy? Could recycling of OPEC surpluses be handled so smoothly if the Euro-currency markets were subject to greater control, and, in particular, would it be more difficult to accommodate the financing needs of the developing countries? Would OPEC countries be willing to accumulate large holdings of financial assets if the Euro-currency markets were regulated by national authorities? And if they were not willing, what would the consequences be, especially for the volume of petroleum some of those countries would be willing to produce and export?

7. One of the most urgent national requirements is the need to construct and carry out a sensible domestic energy program. There also is a need to construct a parallel and compatible international program. A start has been made by some intergovernmental consultations on the subject among the major oil importing nations, but much remains to be done.

In this regard, one of the issues to be faced is whether an international program should be limited to *importers* of oil and have as its objective a united front vis-à-vis the oil exporters, or should the program, if at all possible, endeavor to bring producer and consuming nations together to reach long-term agreements designed to assure a more stable and dependable flow of oil to market. While the current turmoil in Iran and the disunity among OPEC members on matters of pricing and production ceilings would seem to make the latter course an unrealistic alternative, the effort should be made. With some ingenuity and good fortune, perhaps something worthwhile could be accomplished.

One idea worth exploring is whether, in exchange for long-term supply contracts at negotiated prices, the oil exporters might be offered some form of "maintenance purchasing power" on their future accumulations of financial assets. The design of any such program would have to overcome many technical and political difficulties (such as, for example, the share of each importing nation in the guarantee commitment). Nevertheless, such an approach might be more attractive to all parties than the present turmoil which carries a risk that soaring oil prices may "bankrupt" enough developing nations to create a world-wide financial crisis and depression—a situation that would threaten not only world peace but also the social fabric of both oil-importing and oil-exporting nations.

8. What should be done to improve the political and economic relationships between the United States and the developing countries? The present relationships are marked by animosity on the part of many of those countries. At best, they suspect our government of lack of understanding of their aspirations and needs for preferential access to our market. At their worst, they suspect us of actual hostility. Though their feelings to a considerable extent apply to all the highly developed countries, the United States receives the brunt of their suspicions and complaints. At the same time, the developing countries frequently fail to understand the constraints to which the United States is subject and are unrealistic in their proposals and demands.

Their hostility has found forums for expression in the United Nations, the UN Conference on Trade and Development (UNCTAD), the Economic and Social Council of the UN (ECOSOC), the UN Conference on Science and Technology for Development (UNCSTD), and the International Labor Organization (ILO), among other places. These forums provide not simply a place for venting feelings; they also provide a place where action programs can be conceived and promoted. In fact, increasingly, the developing countries seem to be using these organizations to promote ill-conceived action programs aimed at the highly advanced countries and especially at large American business firms with foreign subsidiaries. The problem is not with action programs per se —it is with the unrealistic and self-defeating nature of many of the specific programs that are being advanced. While the international organizations have no legislative or enforcement powers in the economic sphere, they do influence public opinion, provide technical advice to drafters of national legislation, and in other ways promote the translation of rhetoric into action in the so-called Third World.

What should the response of the United States be to the aggressive efforts of the developing countries to use the international agencies for their ends? At present all too often we neither challenge these efforts very effectively nor channel them toward more positive directions.

The United States does not have a very effective foreign aid program in terms of winning foreign friends and extending U.S. influence. At the same time, our economic and strategic dependence on raw materials from the developing countries is mounting. We need to invest more in these countries, yet relations between them and us are a serious impediment to that.

It is essential that more attention be given to these problems. The initial mishandling of the U.S. government's negotiations with Mexico over the price we would permit American pipeline companies to pay for Mexican gas, and the consequences of that mishandling, are a good illustration of the general problem of poor relationships and the need to improve them.

9. The state of trade relationships between the East and the West is not satisfactory to either side. One of the major problems has been the issue of linkage between trade and other U.S. objectives, such as human rights in Russia. Some have argued that U.S. policies have served mainly to deprive American exporters of opportunities to export to the Soviet-bloc countries and have produced little or no progress in human rights in those countries that could not have been achieved solely by persistent efforts to focus world

opinion on violations of the Helsinki Accord. In any event, the 1979 revision of the Export Administration Act did include provisions which were designed to curb the President's ability (sometimes exercised) to deny export licenses on foreign policy grounds. More recently, the Russian invasion of Afghanistan has placed the future of Soviet-American trade in a new and grimmer context in the short term, and the longer-term relationship may also be affected.

10. The United States is in the midst of international negotiations on a law of the sea treaty. These negotiations cover many issues that, if unresolved, could breed international tensions and even provoke international conflict. One major set of issues relates to rights of passage through waters claimed by one or more nations as being inside their territorial limits. Another set of issues pertains to the rights and responsibilities of those who seek to extract minerals from seabeds lying beyond any nation's territorial limits. The law of the sea negotiations have moved erratically and have encountered many obstacles. Some in the business community fear that any agreement the United States could achieve would be harmful to our long-term economic interest in tapping the mineral resources of the sea and that we would be better off without a treaty than with the kind with which we could get the developing countries to agree. On the other hand, there are some international legal rights this country wants to obtain, especially in the area of rights of passage, that it is said we cannot obtain except as part of an overall law of the sea treaty. In view of the extended period over which law of the sea negotiations have been underway without reaching conclusion, it would seem worthwhile to review our current strategy in these negotiations in the light of current circumstances and of a new assessment of our needs.

11. One of this nation's greatest sources of strength lies in the exceptional productivity of American agriculture. Increasingly the United States is becoming a source of food on which many other nations depend. In fact, some are suggesting that we should use "the food weapon" against OPEC if its members refuse to adopt more moderate pricing practices. And President Carter did curb shipments of grain to Russia in response to that country's invasion of Afghanistan. These developments give greater urgency to the need to review our current agricultural policies in the light of the

international conditions expected to prevail in the 1980s and to inquire whether these policies best serve our international as well as our domestic objectives. Among other things, the review should address the question of the need for stockpiles of agricultural products and other raw materials—their appropriate size and how they should be financed.

12. The United States recently rejoined the International Labor Organization, which we left in 1977 because of dissatisfaction with its behavior. The ILO is actively engaged in many areas of interest to world business and labor, especially in matters of labor standards, human rights, and the responsibilities of employers. Now that the U.S. has rejoined, our government will need to vote on many matters which may well affect the eventual course of labor legislation in many foreign countries, and even quite possibly to some extent here in this country. While the specific issues are too numerous and complex to review here, it is important to note that many of them will require the government to take positions—positions which in some instances will first need to be formed in the public arena at home.

Conclusions

The foregoing list of significant international economic issues facing the United States in the changed world environment is by no means exhaustive, and none of the issues mentioned has been treated in any depth. This is not the occasion to do so. But the list, and the cursory review of each topic on it, will suffice to enable us to draw the two most essential conclusions—the conclusions toward which all the preceding parts of this chapter have been heading.

The first conclusion is that practically none of the issues lends itself very readily to the sorts of discussion and debate that normally occur in presidential campaigns. Each of the issues is technical and complex. Each lends itself much better to treatment by congressional committees and to the President's Economic Report than to campaign formats, especially with the prevailing reliance of political campaigns on brief television appearances and "catchy" generalizations. Moreover, in our pluralistic and issue-oriented society, a successful candidate has little choice but to gloss over technical problems and details and to emphasize broad generalities which will appeal to most voters and antagonize few. One can quite seriously raise the question, therefore, whether any of the specific issues listed above is more likely eventually to be resolved more sensibly as a result of having been fully addressed by any presidential candidate during his campaign than it would be if it had not been so addressed.

This leads to the second and more fundamental conclusion: it is not the individual issues, as such, which need to be dealt with in the campaign. Rather, it is what Americans desire this country's international role to be in the changed world environment, how we can best achieve our goals in this regard, what sacrifices we are willing to make to achieve them, and what demands we are prepared to make of our allies. These are questions which can and need to be addressed in a presidential campaign.

It has been noted that American relative economic power and influence have been declining. How important is it to try to check the decline? What would be the long-term consequences of *not* doing so? What changes in our international policies would be needed and what would the major social and economic costs or trade-offs be? To what extent is improvement in our economic status related to restoration of foreign confidence in our military ability to protect our allies as well as ourselves? To what extent should this nation unabashedly use its economic strength to achieve its political objectives, as most other nations generally do?

What needs to be done domestically? If more emphasis on investment and on savings to finance such investment would be called for, would some social programs have to have their growth curtailed? To what extent is raising the level of investment and the rate of growth of productivity so imperative for international as well as for domestic reasons that we are willing to accept changes in our tax structure which may, at least for a while, result in some change in the distribution of national income (e.g., increase the share of profits)?

At the present time, our domestic policies in many areas tend to be treated as if they had no important consequences for the international competitiveness and strength of the United States. As Alan William Wolff, formerly U.S. Deputy Special Trade Representative, succinctly noted in an address to the Business Economists Club of Cleveland in November 1979, "Thus, decisions are taken on taxation of Americans abroad on grounds of equity, on antitrust questions on grounds of antitrust policy, on export controls on grounds of foreign policy concerns, on environmental controls in terms of air quality, on agents' fees on standards of morality, on aviation policy on grounds of immediate consumer benefits, and so on. And to look at the whole picture of the cumulative impact on U.S. international policy not only cannot easily be done; *it is not attempted.*" (Emphasis added.) This is a situation that can be changed only if the President is determined to bring it about and is willing and able to persuade the public that it is imperative in the new environment to do so.

Clearly, in their campaign speeches, presidential aspirants will try to avoid questions which get into details, and especially ones pertaining to burden-sharing, but they should at least be prepared to address the subject of their perceptions of the importance of halting the decline in our relative international position and of the broad contours of how they would seek to reverse that decline. Once having established the framework, the successful candidate would then be able to have his administration deal with the specific issues on the list in a reasonably consistent and meaningful way. Moreover, in their campaign position papers, candidates should be expected to go into considerable detail on major economic issues.

The two fundamental issues which need to be addressed, therefore, are (a) what should this country's international role be and (b) how should the nation seek to achieve it once it has been defined. How these two issues are treated by Presidents in the 1980s largely will determine not only this nation's international power and influence for many years ahead but also its domestic rate of growth and well-being, and perhaps its security as well.

When the probable consequences of a further decline in the international position of the United States are contemplated, the prospect is disturbing. Is world peace at all secure if the world becomes increasingly fragmented, with each nation or bloc guided primarily by immediate self-interest? Yet this is what seems to be happening, and the trend is being accelerated by the scramble of a number of countries for "assured" access to Middle East oil supplies. There is a need for strong international leadership by some nation—leadership exercised in accordance with principles recognized by most as being in the interest of all. This is the kind of leadership the United States supplied immediately following World War II. The need is no less now. And there is no other nation even remotely capable of assuming the role.

The United States cannot regain such a role, however, until it has substantially raised its rate of productivity growth, which in turn will require considerably more attention to promoting investment and technological advance, and until it has brought inflation under control. Finally, it must also greatly reduce its dependence on foreign oil. When these three objectives have been achieved, our balance of payments will be healthy and the dollar once again will be a strong currency no longer requiring periodic large-scale assistance from other countries' central banks. A strong dollar is an essential requirement for international economic leadership by the United States.

Clearly, the objective of the United States cannot and should not be to restore the degree of economic predominance we inherited at the end of World War II. That degree of dominance was possible only because of the physical exhaustion of Europe, Russia, and Japan and the weakness of China. Nevertheless, a return to a substantial position of international economic leadership and respect is possible. The goals of world peace, stability, and economic growth all would be served if the United States were to regain some of the ground it has lost as a consequence of its economic performance during the past decade.

In addition, the military position of this country needs to be kept strong. No country can provide real economic leadership without having corresponding military strength because a country which lacks the power to protect its economic interests when they are attacked by others cannot long hold its economic position.

In fact it can be said that without power—both military and economic—there can be no meaningful U.S. international economic policies. The very essence of policy is the ability to influence events and affect the outcome of events. But without some degree of power, a country cannot affect events—it is driven by events. Both in economic and political matters, countries will follow the leadership of that country which is perceived to be able most to affect the course of world events.

But more than that, a world in which there is no clear leader is one which is not likely to be able to preserve the considerable progress toward freer trade and investment, economic development of poorer countries, and generally high rates of growth achieved in the two decades following World War II. In this connection, it may be instructive to review the period between World War I and World War II, a period in which no single country was able or willing to assume international leadership, and inquire whether this lack of leadership does not explain much of what went wrong in that period and the sorry events which followed.

The real choice facing the United States would seem not to be whether the country needs to endeavor to improve its weakened international position but rather the degree of urgency to be attached to the goal and the measures best suited to achieve it. This is a theme on which presidential aspirants can and should debate.

Simon Ramo

6

The U.S. Technology Slip:

A New Political Issue

Ours is a highly technological society and all nations of the world, developed and underdeveloped, now perceive their economic strength as highly dependent on their technological prowess. Already more than one aspiring U.S. presidential candidate has lamented the slowdown of technological advance in the U.S. and identified this shortcoming as one cause of inflation, unemployment, declining productivity, trade deficits, weakened security posture, and a general downturn in our international position. This political attention is not surprising, because wide concern is building in the U.S. that our innovative and entrepreneurial spark is dying as, in area after area, our traditional lead is being usurped by other nations.

SIMON RAMO *is the "R" and a cofounder of TRW, Inc. He has been chief scientist of the nation's Intercontinental Ballistic Missile Program, chairman of the President's Committee of Science and Technology, and a member of the Advisory Committee to the Secretary of State for Science and Foreign Affairs and the Advisory Council to the Secretary of Commerce. Dr. Ramo, a member of the National Academy of Sciences, is also a trustee and visiting professor in management science at the California Institute of Technology and fellow of the faculty of the Kennedy School of Government of Harvard.*

The U.S. technology slip was bound to become a political issue because lethargy regarding scientific research and technological development is especially penalizing to the U.S. society, where the economy, sense of values, and social structure are strongly based on a generous availability of the fruits of employing these disciplines. Political pundits assure us that no approach to our social and economic problems is politically viable if it contemplates the average citizen's acceptance of significantly reduced supplies of goods and services. It is also politically unrealistic to expect those now disadvantaged to abandon their aspirations for the higher living standards the majority enjoys. If these are political truths, then the tools of science and technology must be sharpened and applied vigorously since such action is indispensable for a feasible approach to national problems.

Whether the objective is lowering the cost of national security or increasing productivity for nonmilitary segments of the economy, the technological advance route offers real hope for progress. If the voter will not countenance lowered supply, then we must look for ways to increase supply while using the same human resources. If natural resources are dwindling, then we must learn how to synthesize more resources economically. Scientific research, if avidly pursued, can teach us how to apply the laws of nature more effectively. Technology can be employed more broadly to develop additional economically advantageous products whose production would create new jobs to fight unemployment. Further efforts can lead us to lower costs as a counter to inflation, substitutes for materials in short supply, and ways to provide for our needs with less harm to the environment. There is only one way for the people of the United States to have a generally higher standard of living and to increase the flow of goods and services to those well below the average partaker. This is by increasing the quantity and quality of what we produce, an appropriate and practical role for technology.

But these are merely possibilities. Are we implementing them? Are we in the United States using science and technology to the fullest on behalf of our society? This is not to ask whether we are following up every clue to nature's undiscovered secrets and constructing every machine it is technically possible to build. These latter are very different and less serious questions. We are inquiring, rather, if our scientific and technological know-how is being applied properly where there is strong evidence of high economic and social rewards for the effort. To this important question the answer is *no*. We are becoming slower, more timid, and less innovative in applying science and technology.

Of course, even if we were to attain perfection in the selection and implementation of technological programs, we still would not be guaranteed a healthy economy and a happy society. If we handle nontechnological matters badly we can have unemployment, inflation, and other economic ills all at once. However, without a strong technological foundation our economic and social needs cannot be satisfied. Science and technology are not sufficient, but they are necessary.

They are essential to the U.S. for more than domestic tranquility. International economic competitiveness by the U.S. and our contribution to world stability and progress both hinge on the status of our science and technology. If world economic health is fostered by each nation's supplying what it best can to other nations and trading with them for their most suitable items in return, then continuing advances in science and technology by the U.S. are fundamental to doing our part.

How serious is the U.S. technology slip? What real evidence exists that we are getting behind, aside from the common sense conclusions one arrives at by noticing the Japanese and European cars on the streets and the televisions, radios, and tape recorders at home.

To begin with, let us look at a measure most commonly cited when concern is expressed: the lagging productivity rise in America. For many decades the U.S. steadily increased its overall national productivity. We led the world in inventing improved techniques and processes and building ever improved plants and equipment. We left other nations far behind, and yet our productivity grew year after year. All this was true up until the last decade.

By 1980 the U.S. had managed to become not first, but last, in the listing of annual rate of productivity growth of the world's industrialized nations. Our annual productivity increases hover around zero while all other nations—France, Italy, the United Kingdom, Japan, and Germany (particularly the last two)—are registering positive productivity gains. From the mid-1940s until the mid-1960s, U.S. productivity increased over 3 percent per year. Then between the mid-1960s and the mid-1970s the annual rate of increase dropped to just over 2 percent. For the last half of the 1970s this rise sank to 1 percent, with a negative figure on our report card as we started the 1980s. All in all, from 1950 to the present time, productivity in Japan rose at a rate four times as fast as the U.S. average increase. In the mid-1960s it took some twenty-five man-hours to produce a ton of steel in a Japanese mill, while the labor required per ton in the United States was half that amount. By the mid-1970s the U.S. figure improved to ten man-hours, but Japan's came down to nine.

During the first half of the 1970s compensation per hour in the U.S. increased about 8 percent per year while productivity increased about 1.5 percent per year. Salaries, wages, and fringe benefits constitute the major components in the cost and prices of all goods and services produced. To the extent that labor costs rise faster than productivity, the difference must find its way into prices. The diminishing rate of productivity has thus not been helpful in fighting inflation. To show the size of the effect in recent years, take 1978 as an example. In that year, a typical American family had five-thousand dollars less income than it would have had if the growth in productivity had not slowed from historic levels. The total loss in goods and services that could have been available to the citizens of America, had we maintained the productivity increases of the mid-1940s, was three hundred billion dollars in 1978 alone, well above the entire defense budget for the year plus the cost of all automobiles purchased.

A glance at our deteriorating trade balance gives us as much cause for alarm as what is happening to our productivity. In 1978 the U.S. trade deficit reached a record of about thirty billion dollars. It is often stated that this was the result of our having imported so much oil at newly raised prices. But in 1978 the U.S. imported 25 percent of the total energy it consumed while Japan imported 95 percent and Germany 60 percent of their respective total energy requirements. In the same year, however, Japan enjoyed a sixty-three billion dollar surplus in manufactures, West Germany, a forty-nine billion dollar surplus, while the U.S. experienced a deficit of about ten billion dollars in that category. Thus the number one problem for us is not that we have to import oil, although that hurts us, but rather that we apparently are no longer very effective at converting materials and energy into manufactured goods when compared with these other nations. They have taken both the world and our domestic markets away from us in substantial part. If they were not superior in manufacturing, then their adverse situation compared with ours in energy imports would have caused them to experience serious trade deficits. Instead it is we who have them.

We are now importing manufactures at 2.5 times the rate of oil. Our biggest loss of trade position has been in that category of trade labeled "mechanical systems." This represents about 75 percent of our trade. It includes heavy machines, light machines, cars and trucks, and aircraft (plus spacecraft). Only in the last category do we remain relatively strong, with exports around eight billion dollars and essentially no imports. (This favorable situation may not last, however, because the Japanese and Europeans are working hard on plans to invade this market strongly during the 1980s.) In automobiles and trucks we are now importing more than we export by almost twelve billion dollars; in entertainment electronics we are off by four billion dollars; in heavy machinery, by over six billion dollars. In light machinery represented by or used to manufacture most consumer goods—typewriters, clothing, furniture, cameras, etc.—we are showing a deficit of over twelve billion dollars. The total deficit of the U.S. in trade machinery and all the products based on that machinery is some thirty-five billion dollars. This means we are losing the jobs associated with essential, clean industry and its accompanying tax base, aggravating our balance of payment problems and failing to ease the economic impact of importing so much oil.

Let us leave this incomplete recital of evidence of our slipping badly in technological development to speculate on some of the reasons for this slip. As we look at the possible causes we shall find additional evidence that the technological lag we are developing is serious and can easily worsen.

Part of our growing disadvantage in manufactured goods is investment in research and development (R & D) relative to it. In Japan and Germany the R & D budgets, while individually lower than ours in absolute terms, are more heavily concentrated on the engineering that goes directly to productivity and export advantages. By comparison, our larger R & D expenditures are more heavily concentrated in defense and the meeting of government environmental and safety regulations. Even though it is believed that new technology accounts for some 40 percent of the total effect on productivity increases, the U.S. spent only something like 1.8 percent of its GNP in the 1970s on nondefense R & D while Japan spent 2.1 percent and West Germany spent 2 percent. Private U.S. industry actually employed 5 percent fewer scientists and engineers at the end of the five-year period 1970 to 1975 than at the beginning. It has been reported that for 1979 U.S. manufacturers expected their R & D budgets to equal less than 50 percent of their capital investment budgets. In the mid-1960s this figure was closer to 80 percent.

Of course, no precise way exists to measure the impact of technological advance on overall real economic growth or even on productivity growth. However, most who have studied this problem intensively have estimated that technology advance is responsible for between 25 to 50 percent of the growth of the American economy in the last several decades. About 75 percent of our manufactured goods exports have been technologically intensive, and 50 percent of our manufactured imports are in this category. If agricultural products are counted as technological—with our mechanical equipment, fertilizers, pesticides, and preservatives, this is a realistic categorization—then the impact of technology on our exports is well over 75 percent.

We are also low in capital investment, the other major influence on productivity increases. If we deduct from the figures for capital investment backing up each worker in the U.S. that part of the investment made to comply with pollution and safety regulations, the net investment (expressed as a ratio to value added during the manufacturing operation under consideration) has declined in the manufacturing sector of the U.S. economy since 1967. The capital per worker actually went down from $258 per worker in 1967 to $220 per worker in 1973. In the same period this indicator rose from $298 to $693 in West Germany and from $191 to $324 in Japan. Overall the U.S. invests only 15 percent of its GNP; West Germany, 22 percent; and Japan, 29 percent.

Applied research and development in U.S. industry, whether through government sponsorship (as in military, space, and nuclear energy) or private investments (to develop new products and manufacturing techniques), has not kept pace with inflation over the last decade. The actual expenditure in such R & D as a fraction of GNP has fallen from over 3 percent to just over 2 percent. During this period the R & D budgets (again as a ratio of the nation's overall domestic product) rose in France and Germany. If we look carefully at the makeup of our R & D programs as compared with other developed nations, we discover that the decline in R & D in the United States has resulted almost entirely from cutbacks in defense, space, and nuclear R & D, all sponsored by the government, and not from private R & D decreases. Apparently in view of the negative U.S. results in productivity and trade, our industrial R & D is not well focused on those aspects of technology which have most to do with improving these two performance indicators.

The government provides us with figures showing the fraction of U.S. patents granted each year to foreigners. This fraction has doubled in the last ten years. In the past five years, foreigners have been awarded more than 33 percent of all the patents issued by the United States government. The share of patents held by Americans abroad has substantially declined. In the 1950s over 80 percent of the major inventions brought to market in the U.S. were developed in the United States. By the late 1960s the figure had declined to just over 50 percent. Both continuous casting and the basic oxygen process for the making of steel were refined in Japan. Disk brakes and radial tires appeared on European cars before they were introduced into the United States. British scientists invented both the hip replacement device that has helped so many victims of arthritis and the CAT scanner which has revolutionized medical diagnosis. The French pioneered the discovery of the phenothiazine drugs that have radically altered treatment of psychotic patients. Studies have been made of the source of the most significant technological advances, and, whereas a decade or so ago the U.S. seemed to dominate the list, more recently other nations have been first in an increasing number of areas.

Until the late 1960s, a large number of new U.S. technological corporations were founded each year based on technological innovation. After that time stock issues to launch such entrepreneurial enterprises dropped to a trickle. In the last year or two some recovery has occurred, but the activity remains well below the earlier levels. Such a fall-off should be a source of concern about creativity and competitiveness in the utilization of science and technology in the U.S. when we consider that the key ideas for the following fields came from individuals who were not employed in large organizations: atomic energy, advanced electrical batteries, computers, cellophane, color photography, the cyclotron, DDT, FM radio, foam rubber, inertial guidance, insulin, lasers, the polaroid camera, radar, rockets, streptomycin, the vacuum tube, zerography, and the zipper. It is true that the bulk of industrial R & D is done by the top 100 largest technological corporations. However, a loss of the contributions from innovative small entities is bound to be penalizing.

But if conspicuous evidence exists to suggest we are losing our leadership in technology, there is a lot to say we are still ahead on points in the pure science olympics even if we do not win every event. We have more Nobel laureates than the rest of the world combined. We are still ahead in solid state technology (where we were first with the transistor) and large-scale integrated circuits (complex electronic circuitry on tiny chips). This applies as well to digital computers, digital communications, and virtually every other aspect of information technology. Continued leadership in this field has strong implications for productivity improvements. This is because microminiaturized electronic circuitry now makes feasible very low price and reliable man-machine information systems, greatly expanding our ability to handle information and making each of us smarter at our job. Since information is basic to every pursuit of man in business, industry, government, the professions, and transportation, leadership in information technology by the U.S. bodes well for our economy.

Similarly, even though the Soviet Union holds the world record for the largest number of continuous hours a man has spent in a space capsule, we have on the whole accomplished much more in putting apparatus into space reliably and using the capabilities of such apparatus effectively in cooperation with ground systems. We landed men on the moon and brought them back safely, while the Soviet Union was in difficulty trying to land pieces of equipment to measure and radio back some data. Our communications, earth observation, weather, and solar system research spacecraft surpass U.S.S.R. performance in these areas.

In agriculture, we are blessed with a combination of terrain, soil, weather, water, mechanical equipment, fertilizers, pesticides, food

preservatives, packaging, and distribution techniques that are substantially superior to the agricultural resources of other nations.
Moreover, we have a store of additional ideas in process that, from
seed to mouth, should greatly increase our potential to be a world
exporter of food, this at a time when the rest of the world will
need it as much as we all seem to need petroleum today.

However, there is some bad news on the pure research front. This
kind of research, largely sponsored by government and accomplished by universities, has suffered from shrinking budgets in the
late sixties and early seventies and expanding bureaucracy since
then. Even though the trend to lower research budgets was reversed
by the Ford administration (a reversal fortunately continued by
Carter), nevertheless, after compensating for inflation and the enormously added administrative requirements that now accompany
research grants, U.S. basic research effort is seen not to have kept
pace as a fraction of the nation's GNP. Such research, generally
regarded by everyone as the planting of seeds for future technological advance and long-run improved economic strength, is increasing in other countries. Our failure to support more pure
research does not explain our recent drop in productivity growth,
but it is setting up for future technological weakness and is just as
disturbing.

Returning to the listing of causes for our slippage, it is worth
examining our productivity shortcomings further. Usually, when
productivity is discussed quantitatively, the concept of efficiency
dominates. As to efficiency per se (output divided by input), no
doubt exists that we are slipping badly. While efficiency is not the
only criterion of success in applying science and technology to our
national goals, it is important. But as a matter of national goals
we may be willing to sacrifice efficiency if it gives us something we
want that we would otherwise not get—for example, less pollution.
We are willing to produce fewer shoes per worker per year if it
yields us the privilege of walking barefoot on a clean beach. We are
willing to trade efficiency in the number of parts we produce per
year if a drop in that rate means less danger to the worker in the
process of manufacture.

Now, it is one thing to tolerate inefficiency because we want to
gain something which is unattainable if we allow efficiency to control everything. It is another to be inefficient merely because we

are backward, or because we inadvertently put barriers in the way of innovative effort, or fail to create inducements for the investments we seek. If we become inefficient enough we will lose the option to reach the very social goals we have chosen because we see them as superior to blind technological advance. When we decide to increase safety for the workers and those who will use the produced products, we will have to invest to achieve that aim. It costs something to find out how to be safer. We may have to buy new facilities and equipment to cut safety hazards. We may have to use more man-hours to achieve the same output. Those funds and efforts could have gone instead into making the operation more efficient, turning out more products with fewer man-hours. We face the choice of either being safer or more productive. Similarly, if we invest to limit impairment of the environment from production operations, then again we will be using resources which could have gone into productivity improvement instead. There is again a trade-off: less pollution versus higher productivity. If the nation's sense of values and balancing of factors has been correct, we should have no reason to be concerned about any U.S. productivity slip that can be attributed to this specific set of national goals.

If our productivity falls far enough, then U.S. industry will lose out in both domestic and world markets. Unemployment will rise, living standards will diminish, the poor will get poorer, and illness will rise. But do we have good means to effect trade-off compromises? It has been claimed that those who set safety and environmental standards have never even considered the related productivity or cost problems, let alone attempted a careful balancing. A slight lowering of standards might keep a given hazard still within a sensible range while at the same time almost eliminating the productivity drop overly severe standards may have caused.

Many other interactions of technology with social goals affect U.S. productivity and our overall technological stature. For example, one way to turn out more per man-hour is to have superior workers. But what about the untrained and, hence, the unemployable? How do we change the society to remove the seemingly permanent membership in it of a substantial number of disadvantaged, unskilled, frustrated people? One way is to make it a national goal that our productive system must pay the added price of including them now as apprentices and trainees so that later they may become full-fledged, skilled employees. Surely this will mean a sacrifice of productivity in the interim, a period stretching out for years. Despite lowering the nation's productivity statistics, such a program might yield real benefits. It is better for a worker to receive $200 per week in pay even if the $200 comes partially from taxing everybody to subsidize that worker's modest contribution while he is learning than to pay him the same $200 in unemployment relief while he is idle and learning nothing.

As another example, when we alter a manufacturing process so as to use less energy even if it requires more man-hours—a substitution of labor for energy—we lose in productivity, but we gain in the national goal of being free of domination by the OPEC countries.

Precisely because hurting productivity may be a necessary, though not highly cherished, corollary to achieving certain high priority objectives, it is important that we stop impairing productivity and constraining technological development where such handicaps buy us no progress toward any perceived goals. We may not want more food produced and marketed if it has to be done by the use of those fertilizers, pesticides, or preservatives that would increase the cancer rate. On the other hand, we do not want people to be deprived of adequate nutrition. That means producing as much safe food as possible at the lowest price. We need more homes and more jobs, and it is not obvious that more workers building more houses has to result in significantly more pollution. If we could develop our creative, analytical, and discriminatory capabilities to the level of being able to separate well the desirable from undesirable technological efforts, then we could hope to have our cake and eat it too. The more we can prevent the wrong efforts, the more human and natural resources we will have available to put into the right efforts.

When it comes to doing the right things as against the wrong ones, it is encouraging that no evidence has surfaced to suggest that Americans are now basically any less innovative than in previous decades or centuries. "Yankee ingenuity" is as applicable to the South and to the North, to the city dwellers and the farmers, to recent immigrants and early settlers. If there is now less manifestation in America of inventiveness and ambition to break new ground, it must be because something about the pattern of our society today is creating too many obstacles, providing too little motivation, and generally creating the wrong environment. Here, I am afraid we have more bad news.

In the U.S. the biggest concentration of expertise that can give us the benefits of technological innovation resides in the private sector. Here one finds experience and know-how in applying science and technology to the requirements of the society. The industry has systems for arranging financial backing and experienced management to carry out successful implementations. Unfortunately, this private contribution sector has in recent years had less funds available for backing innovative technology than is desirable. It has had more regulation from government than the society probably intended, even granted a sound interest in superior standards regarding safety, health, and environmental protection.

The most straightforward and important limitation on technological innovation in American industry is a lack of adequate cash flow. We could state this in various other ways. We could say that the real return on investment is not good enough, or that the reward-to-risk ratio has deteriorated. We could point to the fact that out of every dollar of reported earnings some sixty cents goes to taxes. Then some twenty cents must go to providing for true replacement costs, since IRS rules do not allow the real costs of depreciation. Then if, of the remaining twenty cents, fifteen cents is put out as dividends to the shareholders (who consider that amount too little to jump at the chance for further investment), this leaves only five cents for improving the operation, developing new products, increasing productivity, and adjusting to the myriad of new safety and pollution rules. We could also sum it up by saying that the critical limitations on technological innovation in the United States consist of inflation, disincentive taxing policies, and over-regulation. The government is rather heavily involved in all three of these factors.

Improving the environment and increasing safety in the production and use of products are meritorious objectives of the society, and the government has a necessary function to perform here. However, recent studies have indicated that government regulations in 1978 alone cost industry over one hundred billion dollars. That means those funds were not available for technological innovation to increase productivity or to produce new products, create jobs, and compete internationally so as to improve our trade balances. Some of these expenditures were for safety, environmental, and other purposes totally consistent with the desires of the American citizenry. Equally without doubt, however, is that a sum so huge includes much needless regulation. It covers expenses in altering methods and buying apparatus to make these alterations possible, to achieve very questionable or negligible improvements in many instances. It also funds a huge amount of bureaucratic administration on the part of both industry and the government regulatory apparatus.

We wanted to increase safety and cut pollution, but we have been slow in working out common sense balances in the process and have produced a structure costly beyond the intended levels.

Without meaning to do so, our regulatory climate discourages innovation in new product areas. Even beneficial regulation, to ensure compliance with sound standards, is bound to cause R & D to become more concentrated on lesser-risk projects, those where regulatory problems in bringing out the product are less likely to arise. Unfortunately, the more innovative a new program, the greater the business risk. More new ideas turn out to be impractical when the details of the real-life market are uncovered than those that mature successfully. Regulations create delays and uncertainties on top of the meeting of conventional return on investment criteria. Every embryonic project being considered must be seen now as able to pass safety and environmental hurdles not easy to define and anticipate well ahead. The easy route to take is to play safe, putting available chips on incremental improvements and avoiding a try for bigger steps.

Under these circumstances, it is small wonder fewer new technological corporations are being started compared with a decade ago. It is a far more risky business now to start a new company based on innovative ideas. The novel product may be welcomed by the market, but the cost of doing business will be higher and the return on investment lower than realistically could be assumed in former years. Investors are more inclined now to be leery of speculative technological developments.

Now, how does all this relate to presidential campaigns? America's lagging technological innovation has been discovered by the politicians so the candidates may offer suggestions as to how to put

America back into a technology leadership position. To many citizens and some candidates, when a serious national problem surfaces, the proposed solution is for the government to stay out and let the free market take care of it. To them, allowing the government to get into anything means the problem will worsen. They see the government as an enormously wasteful, incompetent, inefficient bureaucracy. To perhaps an equal, or maybe larger, number of others, government action is the only answer. As they see it, business, particularly big business, cannot be objective, cannot make decisions in the national interest, but will act only on behalf of the narrow goals of shareholders and mainly for short-term profit maximization.

In actuality, a large fraction of all the most important areas of technology already involves the government heavily, with little chance of a truly free market's being an available route. Business leadership will not make investments unless they see an environment for a satisfactory return-to-risk ratio. This they do not expect, not when the area of endeavor has become highly politicized and the government is expected to be much in the act.

For example, by all-out use of science and technology, and the full cooperation of government and private industry, we could have a plentiful supply of energy for hundreds of years by properly utilizing our huge reserves of coal. Existing technology beginnings can be advanced to desulfurize coal, produce liquid and gaseous fuel from it, mine it more safely, obtain a good deal of energy from it without mining (in situ), and burn it more cleanly and fully to limit environmental harm. The resulting energy supply would be higher priced than today's oil, in part to write off the cost of the technological advance, but the payments would stay in the United States. Those who have studied the problem tell us that the gains of the strong economy which adequate energy would help ensure would exceed the negative impact on GNP of the higher price for that energy.

Success in such an approach requires both the know-how of private industry and enormous capital placed at risk. A profit-seeking corporation choosing to make a major entry into synthetic gas or liquid fuel from coal by new technology would have to commit funds in the billions of dollars. Decades might pass before a return on that investment could be realized. Indeed such return might never eventuate, so great are the risks associated with unpredictable government decisions on critical aspects. The complete system needed for a much greater utilization of coal in the U.S. involves a host of private and public organizations that are semi-autonomous and not readily directed by any one body (not even the White House or Congress): landowners, mine operators, labor unions, railroads, power generating and water supply utilities, numerous engineering and manufacturing organizations, county and state governments, and many, many agencies in the federal government that deal with prices, environment, labor, antitrust, and transportation, to name only a portion.

Under such circumstances, a totally private sector approach to greatly enhanced use of coal is an unlikely path.

We could readily provide similar rationale with regard to development of ocean resources, the fullest use of our present leads in space technology and information technology, and even the maximizing of our unique situation in agriculture. The exploiting of sweeping technological advances will all involve a hybrid of private sector and government actions, only slightly cooperative, often confrontational, and increasingly political. Now that technological innovation is appreciated as basic to a strong economy and as a political issue, it may be expected that two sides will develop. One set of political candidates will claim the route to more technological innovation is to get the government out of the act and allow the free market full reign. This would certainly mean espousing the complete abandonment of price controls and allocations and a major redo of our regulatory policies and bureaucratic apparatus. Another group will advocate more government programs.

Some influential people in and out of government have pushed for some time for massive government programs to enhance the status of technology in the United States. Well, why not have the government do more—beyond such projects as a rocket to the moon, intercontinental ballistic missiles, fusion nuclear power, and breeder reactors—projects that free enterprise cannot perform alone? Why not have the government embark on a giant effort to increase innovation and productivity in America by all-out development of new technology? To go this far, to have the government move into direct technological advance, even into those segments where private enterprise is still strong and willing, would take the government right into the heart of the functioning of the free market. Would that help the nation?

Technological advance is infinite in its varieties and dimensions. The new products that conceivably could be developed, the changes in production methods that are technically possible, and the inventable alterations of virtually every system of producing, distributing, and using technical products and services are endless in number. The nation has the resources, technically trained people, and funding to back them up, to carry through only a tiny percentage of all that can be thought up. The trick is to choose the right research and development and to assign the limited resources to best meet the citizens' desires and needs. Nothing about government, in theory or past practice, suggests it would be effective in sensing the market's real requirements, the consumers' true wants. Even those who are convinced the free market is an inadequate means for obtaining the proper mesh of resources-to-goals in every aspect of technology usually grant that, if this match is attempted by the federal government instead, the result can only be worse. It would require the creation of a huge government department for multitudinous planning, selection of projects, and detailed assignment of manpower and physical resources.

This does not mean the government should do nothing about technological innovation. Doubtless the government could justify improved research programs in the universities, particularly more support for university programs in advanced production technology, an area where the U.S. lags behind Germany and Japan. In industrial technological innovation, however, the government can help most not by funding more efforts, which simply takes funds out of the private sector, but by cutting inflation and improving the general economy so the private sector will have the financial means and incentives to perform more R & D of its own choice. Licking inflation, lowering capital gains taxes, and decreasing the taxation (presently double) on dividends would especially encourage investment in innovation. Germany's and Japan's investment ratios are much higher than ours and so are their productivity increases. Their capital gains taxes are zero.

Candidates for the Presidency seeking to take stands on what is to be done about America's slipping technological strength would do well to foster neither of the two extreme views: free enterprise alone can do everything best; free enterprise is bad and the government must do everything. If the citizenry are interested in the flexibility, freedom of opportunity, motivation, and incentives of free enterprise, then they need to recognize that free enterprise can only contribute to the nation's needed R & D if private industry is allowed to generate the necessary funds for investment. It would be refreshing to have a presidential candidate who explains that profit is a way of representing the cost of capital. Unless that cost is paid, no capital investment will occur. If there is no capital investment in the private sector, then everything that needs doing will have to be done by the government. If everything is done by the government, then this means government control of production, which in turn requires government allocation of material and human resources, which leads to a totally government-controlled society, which means the government will assign us all to jobs and areas in which to live. Ultimately, we will lose all individual freedom while everything about our lives is arranged by a government bureaucracy.

What should be explained and espoused by presidential candidates, if we are serious about using science and technology more fully on behalf of the nation, is that ours is of necessity a hybrid society, part free enterprise, and part government control. The name of the game is to assign the proper roles and missions to each and then get on with meeting the nation's goals. No single, simple formula for allocation of responsibilities between the two sectors is sensible. It has to be organized and arranged to suit the area of endeavor.

Let us illustrate this, and at the same time sum up the situation on technological innovation, by taking one specific example. It is in the field of energy, but more specifically it is the question of what should be the roles of government and the private sector in the creation of a synthetic fuel industry (from coal or shale) for the United States. It is also the issue of whether or not synthetic fuel is an option deserving an extraordinary priority of attention and investment.

The creation of a synthetic fuel industry on a major scale in the United States is certainly a controversial topic. First of all, there are a lot of alternatives, each with its strong advocates. For instance, we could mount a much more effective program to modify our homes, factories, transportation systems, and the rest so as to greatly conserve energy. Many are convinced that a much smaller investment in conservation than in synthetic fuels would save millions of barrels a day, an amount of production hard to reach with synthetic fuel plants. Moreover, synthetic fuel is a dirty process and numerous critics argue we can never arrive at high outputs without an unacceptable level of pollution. Still others believe that the mere removal of all price controls and allocations by government would cause us to discover more oil on American land or off our shores or elsewhere in the world and would trigger the application of advanced technology to greatly increase the available reserves from existing oil wells in the United States.

There are, of course, the solar enthusiasts. They are confident that if solar energy R & D is accelerated in all its dimensions—from direct sunlight utilization in solar panels in homes and buildings to biomass, the harnessing of the winds and tides and ocean-thermal energy—then we could obtain at least as much as we could get from a tolerable number of synthetic fuel plants. Synthetic fuel from shale and coal is also attacked as putting an undue burden on our water supply problems and on our transportation systems. Moreover, there are those who believe that when the emotional reaction to the Three Mile Island accident has been properly responded to, and some of nuclear energy's least informed critics have moved on to other things, then it will be seen that the nuclear route is the cleanest, safest, and most economical way to supply our energy needs.

The trouble is that none of these alternatives is a sure thing. It is one thing to urge we go on a crash basis for synthetic fuel, violating reasonable environmental standards and neglecting alternatives in the process. It is another to ban entirely synthetic fuel from coal and shale.

Accordingly, let us assume it would be a sensible plan to provide ourselves with the option of synthetic fuel, to go quickly part of the way in synthetic fuel development, refine the know-how, and complete the tryouts so that we can move fast on a next step of high production if we so choose, or can let synthetic fuel rest at an intermediate level if other approaches turn out better. How can we best arrange for synthetic fuel projects along these lines? What are the appropriate roles for government and the free market, or private sector?

To start answering these questions, suppose we first recognize that the government has little competence with which to direct a large-scale technological effort. To be sure, the government can attract a few outstanding people for the top jobs whenever it embarks on a mammoth project, but as to overall expertise, there will be no comparison in competence to lay out, supervise, and bring to success a synthetic fuel project between those the government can recruit as in-house engineers and managers and those American technological industry can assemble. Let us next observe that if the government is to control and fund a synthetic fuel development in its entirety, it must get the funds out of the private sector somehow. When those funds are extracted, that means they are not available there to invest in synthetic fuel (or anything else).

With these two thoughts in mind, let us now discuss a specific proposal. It is not the same as the synthetic fuel program pressed by the Carter administration. It is not to create a government program, involving around one hundred billion dollars, to totally control, fund, and direct synthetic fuel development. Instead, I propose the government announce that, for the government's own use, it wants to purchase a substantial amount of synthetic fuel to be made from coal or shale. The government's requests for proposals will specify a number of important conditions. The government will wish to purchase at the lowest price. The government will promise a ten-year contract for purchase at that price, with a price adjustment factor for inflation during that period. The government will state the quality and nature of the fuel it wishes to purchase and propose a delivery schedule. It might have a formula for deciding on the winners with credit being given both for low price and early start on deliveries. The government will set down some standards as to safety and pollution that it will agree not to tighten without upward price adjustment (cost plus). The government will plan to obtain its requirements—say of the order of a half to a million barrels of oil a day equivalent—from at least two sources. The government will provide immunity from antitrust if companies wish to create a joint venture to bid on the proposal. The government will provide a generous cancellation fee if it wishes to cancel part way through the ten-year period. The government might announce a ceiling price on bids. Clearly the government will have to allow substantial time, perhaps a year, for preparation of the bids.

It is submitted that if the government were to issue this request for bids, a number of firms of high competence and substantial financial backing would come in with offers. The proposals to meet the government's request would be sensible from the standpoint of the bidders because they would not submit them if they were not. Doubtless, the prices quoted in the proposals would be higher than existing petroleum prices but, from what we already know of the technology and economics, not so high as to vitiate the program. The requirements for access to suitable land and water resources for the coal or the shale would be included in the proposals and ultimate contracts. State or federal land would be made available at particular locations at stated price ranges as part of any deals made. Also, as contingencies in the proposal, approvals from various state and federal agencies would be involved. If the government put its conditions down properly in its original request for bids as regards environmental controls and safety, the possibilities of concurrence by the various federal, state, and county groups concerned would be enhanced, though not guaranteed. Similarly, private suits to block operations even after the signing of contracts again would be more likely to be settled reasonably and in reasonable time as compared with recent performances. The legislation creating the program could include provisions for the designated government agency awarding the contracts to have some of the same powers to accelerate law suits and regulatory approvals that President Carter envisaged for his otherwise quite different Energy Mobilization Board.

If this program were created, it would fully cover the requirement to get started in a meaningful way on synthetic fuel. It would set up the option to broaden the program later or keep it as a low-level program. The worst that could happen, from the standpoint of the government, is that if foreign oil did not rise enough in price during the contract period the government would overpay somewhat for the synthetic oil it would have purchased for its own needs.

From the standpoint of appropriate use of both free enterprise and government, we notice that in this proposal the government is not at all involved in the technology, an area where it has the least contribution to make. The government merely creates a guaranteed minimum market for the output of the private sector. The free enterprise industry makes the investment and takes a conventional business risk, choosing the technology it favors. If it wins the competition, it will direct its program. The government will not. No one has to propose on these programs. Any group that bids presumably will do so believing it has the competence and the financial means to handle the job. It has the privilege of making such estimates and calculations as will cause it to feel that, at the price it sets down, it will realize enough return on investment to justify the risk. If it cannot see an approach that meets sound business criteria, it need not make the offer to be a supplier. If a bid sensible from a business standpoint involves a price so high it should not be accepted by the government, the government need not go ahead.

Let us leave this example to summarize this chapter. We have put forth some of the evidence that suggests the U.S. position in science and technology is deteriorating dangerously. A severe technology slip by the United States carries with it unacceptable economic, social, and political consequences. Accordingly, the status of technological innovation and productivity and the overall science and technology standing of the United States is, or deserves to be, a political issue. We have also examined some of the reasons why other nations are taking the lead in important areas of technology away from the United States. We have concluded that our situation is not the result of some fundamental collapse of our basic innovation capabilities. It is rather to be found in inflation, tax policies, and overregulation, factors in which government policies and actions are dominant. We have further suggested that the answer to the problem is not simply to take the government out of every present involvement with science and technology matters and leave the arena totally to the private sector and free enterprise. Nor is it to turn everything over to the government and foster the removal of funds from the private sector in order to fund a government-directed crash effort to accelerate technological innovation and gain improved productivity. The realistic approach is to recognize that using science and technology fully and intelligently in the national interest involves both free enterprise and government and that the citizens will not trust or desire either free enterprise or government alone to control science and technology. The way to obtain the best results for the United States is to assign proper roles and missions to the private sector and government so the teaming will be most effective for each area of endeavor.

Index

About The American Assembly

The American Assembly was established by Dwight D. Eisenhower at Columbia University in 1950. It holds nonpartisan meetings and publishes authoritative books to illuminate issues of United States policy.

An affiliate of Columbia, with offices in the Graduate School of Business, the Assembly is a national educational institution incorporated in the State of New York.

The Assembly seeks to provide information, stimulate discussion, and evoke independent conclusions in matters of vital public interest.

AMERICAN ASSEMBLY SESSIONS

At least two national programs are initiated each year. Authorities are retained to write background papers presenting essential data and defining the main issues in each subject.

A group of men and women representing a broad range of experience, competence, and American leadership meet for several days to discuss the Assembly topic and consider alternatives for national policy.

All Assemblies follow the same procedure. The background papers are sent to participants in advance of the Assembly. The Assembly meets in small groups for four or five lengthy periods. All groups use the same agenda. At the close of these informal sessions, participants adopt in plenary sessions a final report of findings and recommendations.

Regional, state, and local Assemblies are held following the national session at Arden House. Assemblies have also been held in England, Switzerland, Malaysia, Canada, the Caribbean, South America, Central America, the Philippines, and Japan. Over one hundred thirty institutions have co-sponsored one or more Assemblies.

ARDEN HOUSE

Home of the American Assembly and scene of the national sessions is Arden House, which was given to Columbia University in 1950 by W. Averell Harriman. E. Roland Harriman joined his brother in contributing toward adaptation of the property for conference purposes. The buildings and surrounding land, known as the Harriman Campus of Columbia University, are 50 miles north of New York City.

Arden House is a distinguished conference center. It is self-supporting and operates throughout the year for use by organizations with educational objectives.

The background papers for each Assembly are published in cloth and paperbound editions for use by individuals, libraries, businesses, public agencies, nongovernmental organizations, educational institutions, discussion and service groups. In this way the deliberations of Assembly sessions are continued and extended.

The subject of Assembly programs to date are:

1951——United States-Western Europe Relationships
1952——Inflation
1953——Economic Security for Americans
1954——The United States' Stake in the United Nations
——The Federal Government Service
1955——United States Agriculture
——The Forty-Eight States
1956——The Representation of the United States Abroad
——The United States and the Far East
1957——International Stability and Progress
——Atoms for Power
1958——The United States and Africa
——United States Monetary Policy
1959——Wages, Prices, Profits, and Productivity
——The United States and Latin America
1960——The Federal Government and Higher Education
——The Secretary of State
——Goals for Americans
1961——Arms Control: Issues for the Public
——Outer Space: Prospects for Man and Society
1962——Automation and Technological Change
——Cultural Affairs and Foreign Relations
1963——The Population Dilemma
——The United States and the Middle East
1964——The United States and Canada
——The Congress and America's Future
1965——The Courts, the Public, and the Law Explosion
——The United States and Japan
1966——State Legislatures in American Politics
——A World of Nuclear Powers?
——The United States and the Philippines
——Challenges to Collective Bargaining
1967——The United States and Eastern Europe
——Ombudsmen for American Government?

About The Center for Study
of the American Experience

The Center for Study of the American Experience, Annenberg School of Communications, University of Southern California, seeks to examine the unique fabric of American life and to perform analysis and engage in creative thought on problems and opportunities that have been most influential in shaping America's past and present and will be most likely to define America's future. These objectives are pursued in three ways: (1) The assembling of conferences at the highest level of objectivity and expertise, (2) The production of edited audio and video tapes and publications from these conferences, and (3) The support of visiting distinguished Scholars in Residence.

Topics for conferences are formulated to stimulate the greater community into an awareness of the various aspects of the American experience, the potential benefits of future opportunities, and the possible solutions to existing and emerging problems for America.

The Visiting Scholar Program is designed to provide time for research, writing, or other creative endeavors. Visiting Scholars are encouraged to interact with members of the resident faculty and graduate student body.

DATE DUE